LIVING
SPACES

Design
Is in the
Details

Brad Mee

Sterling Publishing Co., Inc. New York
A Sterling/Chapelle Book

Chapelle, Ltd., Inc.,
  P.O. Box 9252, Ogden, UT 84409
  (801) 621-2777 • (801) 621-2788 Fax
  e-mail: chapelle@chapelleltd.com
  Web site: chapelleltd.com

Library of Congress Cataloging-in-Publication Data

Mee, Brad,
  Design is in the details : living spaces / Brad Mee.
       p. cm.
  "A Sterling/Chapelle book."
  Includes index.
  ISBN 1-4027-1393-2
1. Living rooms. 2. Interior decoration. I. Title.

NK2117.L5M44 2005
747.7'5--dc22   005012305

Gen Fund 12/05 _ $25.00

10 9 8 7 6 5 4 3 2 1

Published by Sterling Publishing Co., Inc.
387 Park Avenue South, New York, NY 10016
©2005 by Brad Mee
Distributed in Canada by Sterling Publishing
⅞ Manda Group, 165 Dufferin Street
Toronto, Ontario, Canada M6K 3H6
Distributed in Great Britain by Chrysalis Books Group PLC,
The Chrysalis Building, Bramley Road, London W10 6SP,
England
Distributed in Australia by Capricorn Link (Australia) Pty. Ltd.
P.O. Box 704, Windsor, NSW 2756, Australia
Printed in China
All Rights Reserved

Sterling ISBN 1-4027-1393-2

For information about custom editions, special sales, premium and corporate purchases, please contact Sterling Special Sales Department at 800-805-5489 or specialsales@sterlingpub.com.

CONTENTS

INTRODUCTION   8
ASSESSMENT   10

ROOMS FOR LIVING   12

Living Room   14

Great Room   26

Entertainment Room   34

Special Spaces   40

SURFACES   50

Floors   52

Ceilings   60

Walls   68

SPACE	86	AMENITIES	118
Scale	88	Furniture	120
Light	96	Accessories	138
Color	104	Art	146
Texture	110	Acknowledgments	154
		Credits	156
		Index	159

INTRODUCTION

Take a look at the modern-day living room and you will find an active, vital space that overflows with personality and purpose. However, it hasn't always been this way. Not that long ago it was a stretch using the words "living room" to describe yesterday's stiff parlors and sitting rooms. But times have changed and today's living room has evolved into a lively, space that caters to the activities and interests of its owners while, at the same time, expressing their personal style.

The name and purpose of this room varies from home to home. In some, the space has retained its formality and the title "living room." In others, however, the space is now coined the family room, the media room, the entertainment room, or, a popular catchall, the great room. Capturing the essence of all of these labels, the title "living space" is frequently used to describe this hub of the home. It conveys the purpose of the room in all of its configurations. In every case, it's a space designed for living.

Whether you are in the process of building a new living space, renovating an existing one, or simply looking for ways to bring new life to the one you currently have, creating a vibrant, multifunctional retreat isn't complicated or terribly difficult. You simply need to determine the purpose of the room, decide on a desired style, and provide a heaping dose of detail at every turn. It's best to begin by breaking down your living space and scrutinize its components as you go. This process describes the framework of this book.

We begin with the shell of the room, the structural surfaces that define its boundaries—the floor, ceiling, walls. Consider how large these surfaces are and you'll recognize the opportunity they provide to blanket your living space in your own unique style. Determine of the colors, patterns, and materials that inspire you and turn to them for direction. Also consider the practicality of your material and finish options as each can strongly influence the durability,

sound, and comfort of your room. While you think about the treatment of the surfaces individually, realize that together, they create the foundation of your living space and strongly influence the way it looks and feels.

Once you have dressed the room's surfaces, it is time to take a discerning look at the space they enclose, the actual area of the room. While few living spaces are perfectly proportioned, use detail to alter the way a room feels, the way its roominess is perceived. Whether your living space feels confined and small or overwhelmingly large, your living space can benefit from an informed use of scale, lighting, color, and texture. These design elements can work magic in helping make the most of a room's space while adding to its ambience.

Undoubtedly the most rewarding part of creating a spirited living space is selecting its amenities—the furniture, accessories, art. They bring form, function, and character to the space. With the pieces you choose and the way you place them, your furniture will shape the way the room is actually used, define its activity areas, and affect its comfort level and design direction. With the furniture in place, now apply the finishing touches using accessories and art. From treasured collections to colorful canvases, these elements are vital in creating a room that reflects your personal style and taste. Be creative and indulgent. Remember that while your living room is the most public space under roof, it should make you feel comfortable and at home.

The following chapters are designed to provide the information and inspiration needed to make the most of your home's living room. There are many images and ideas that celebrate detail's power to shape lively, unforgettable living spaces—from large, multi-purpose great rooms to cozy, private nooks. While you will find no single absolute formula, you will discover resourceful ideas and easy-to-follow guides that will help you not only to envision your ideal living room but to make it a reality as well.

ASSESSMENT

Before you begin the exciting process of creating your perfect living space, you should first assess what you now have and determine what you want and need. Take an objective look at your current space. Even if you are building a new room, examining an existing living area will help guide the decisions you make when shaping an entirely fresh space. The evaluation that follows is a three-step process: consider the potential the space offers, identify the characteristics of the room you want to change, and note the design elements you want to keep. The way you want the room to function, look, and feel will naturally influence each step of this evaluation.

ASSESS THE POTENTIAL OF YOUR SPACE

The following questions are designed to help you identify the qualities of a living room that are the most important to you as you evaluate your existing space. They relate to the room's function, form, surfaces, and aesthetics. The exercise of answering these and related questions is essential to evaluating the strength and weakness of your living room and assessing potential for improvement. Once you have done this, you are on your way to creating a welcoming, personalized space that's not only a pleasure to use but also a forum to accommodate your household's activities, enhancing the way in which you live.

- Who currently uses your living space most? Is it under- or overutilized?

- What specific activities take place in your living space? Are there other activities you would like it to accommodate but are unable to because your space doesn't have adequate square footage or amenities?

- Do you like to entertain in your living room? Are your groups of guests large or small? Do you prefer casual get-togethers or formal parties? Does your current space comfortably oblige your gatherings?

- Are there children in the household? Does your living space serve as an active family room where children and their friends gather? What furnishings and features do you have that help an active room perform well? What is missing?

- Do you use your living room for paperwork, reading, or solitary relaxation? Do you have the space, privacy, fixtures, and furniture needed to support these activities?

- Is your current living room isolated from the cooking and dining areas of the home or is it part of a great room? What qualities related to this setup do you most and least enjoy?

- Does your living space allow you to comfortably move around, or are there bottlenecks caused by furniture arrangements?

- Do the room's activity areas conflict with or intrude on each other? Do they seem too closely or broadly spaced?

- Are there existing parts of the room—nooks, insets, bay windows—with space that is not being fully utilized and could be put to better use?

- Are the floor, wall, and ceiling surfaces aesthetically pleasing? Are their materials and treatments practical in areas where they are exposed to pets, children, heavy traffic, and direct sunlight?

- How much maintenance is required for your surfaces? Do you consider this level of care acceptable or unacceptable?

- Does the room feel comfortable? Do family and friends naturally congregate in its space?

- Are the furnishings inviting and relaxing? Are they adaptable, serving multiple purposes in the space?

- Does the room's lighting adequately meet your needs? Is there enough natural sunlight in the room?

- Does your living room seem noisy? Does sound echo in its space?

- Does the room's temperature feel comfortable? Does the room's color and materials contribute to the way it feels—warm or cold?

- Do you enjoy the room's ambience? Does the décor reflect your personal style—casual or formal? Does the décor enhance or diminish the functionality of the room?

IDENTIFY PROBLEM CHARACTERISTICS

Pinpoint what you like and dislike most about your living space. Overlook nothing—large or small. Whether it's the overall size of the room or simply the height at which the light switch rests on the wall, if it affects how you enjoy the room, it is important. Don't concern yourself with determining how to remedy unfavorable elements in the room at this point; for now, simply ascertain what the problems are.

PRIORITIZE THE ROOM'S PROS & CONS

After you have constructed a list of elements you want to keep and those you want to change, prioritize your room's pros and cons. Later you may have to compromise on one element to optimize another. For instance, if you love the open feel of a great room but dislike the noise that can accompany large active spaces, you'll need to identify which quality is more important to you. After all, it's your room and it should perform and feel just as you wish.

RIGHT
This open living space is divided into dining and sitting areas to accommodate the family's casual lifestyle. The dining area's corner window seat was built to provide an additional place to relax.

Today's living room has broad shoulders. Not only is it the most public space under roof, it is also the most multifunctional. We require this vital space to fill a variety of functions: It must be welcoming, comfortable, and aesthetically appealing. It must stand up to the critical eye of visitors as well as the daily use of an active household. In many homes, it must provide and house entertainment systems, possess multiple furniture groupings, feature play areas, and offer special spaces for office work and solitary leisure time. Now that's a heavy burden. To take on all of this, the traditional living room has evolved into many forms.

Some homes function best with a separate living room, dressy or casual, that is removed from other areas of the home. It provides privacy and a separation from the hustle and bustle occurring elsewhere in the home. In many cases, however, homeowners desire a great room that combines living, dining, and cooking zones. Here, the entire family can be together regardless of the individual activities each is enjoying. Some homes also feature specialized entertainment rooms that house media centers, bars, and game tables. And in all of these forms of the living room, people want special spaces that accommodate work and relaxation.

Given the load of activities and elements that shape today's versatile living space, it is imperative that a homeowner first decides on the specific activities the room needs to accommodate. After all, if a room is created around the way a person likes spending time at home, it will be used more frequently and enjoyed much more.

To determine how your living space should take shape, keep track of all that goes on there. If watching TV and listening to music is important, perhaps the room should focus on a built-in media center. If quiet downtime is a prerequisite, soft lighting, comfortable furnishings, and a separation from the home's daily bustle should be incorporated. It all depends on how you prefer living at home.

Once you have outlined the activities that will take place in the room, you can employ dynamic detail to shape and furnish the multitalented living space, giving it a personalized look, and making its tasks and toils seem effortless.

ROOMS FOR LIVING

LIVING ROOM

Do you prefer a living space that is separate from other areas of the home? If so, you are not alone. While the days of the parlor, sitting room, and salon are a thing of the past, many of today's homes still have a living room that sits apart from other areas of the house. This may be by choice or simply because the room is in an older dwelling. In either case, today's separate living room has evolved far beyond its antiquated ancestors. Today's living room is comfortable, stylish, and—above all—used. No longer a stuffy space saved for holidays or a stiff gathering of guests, it welcomes everyday get-togethers with family and friends. Because it is removed from other areas of the home, it also makes a great solitary escape for relaxing with a book. Whatever purpose it serves and whatever name it is given—family room, den, or living room, this separate space is lavished with distinctive detail to make it as inviting and obliging as its modern counterparts' open-floor plans.

FORMAL SPACES

Calm colors, quiet accessories, and soothing furnishings are the modern answer for a formal living room. The separate space serves different purposes for different people. What do you ask of yours? If you want a somewhat formal area that allows you to escape or entertain in style away from the household's chaos, then your décor should differ from that of a living room hosting slumber parties, board games, and evenings of crashing on the sofa with popcorn and movies. After all, activities strongly influence the look and feel of a well-designed living space.

The design and details of today's formal living rooms are less vigorous and spontaneous than that of active family rooms. Color is more calming, accessories less animated, and furnishings less frenzied. The décor is fashioned to suit composed gatherings and quiet downtime alone or with others. While the room may often appear dressed-to-the-nines, it differs from yesterday's ostentatious sitting rooms due to the refreshing detail that embraces it. In this room, comfort and character are never sacrificed for ceremony.

PAGE 15
An infusion of unique materials animate this room. An oversized sofa, distressed leather armchairs, and a large cocktail table provide comfort and richness. A fringed lampshade, pattern-rich pillows, and lively displays of treasured collectibles infuse the space with whimsy and personality.

RIGHT
In this elegant room, matching table lamps, built-in shelves, large seating pieces, and ceiling detail help provide balanced pairings. A few surprises freshen the space: a chaise replaces a matching sofa, three rustic sculptures are boldly displayed, and a bench-like accent piece replaces a more conventional cocktail table.

ABOVE

The ornate carvings and rich finishes of these furnishings and accents infuse a formal room with timeless character and charm. The metallic finish of the orb-filled glass bowl and the chair's nailhead trim add a burnished sparkle to the space.

RIGHT

This end table's boxy form and light finish contrast with the black finish and curvy silhouette of the square cocktail table nearby. The plush, plain-covered sofa and neighboring patterned chair feature different fabrics yet complementary tones.

CREATING A FRESH FORMAL LOOK

In today's home, formal and fresh can work hand in hand. If you seek a more traditionally styled living room with a refined yet updated look, here are a few guidelines to keep in mind.

- Limit the room's disparity in materials and finishes. Select similar wood tones for the tables, chests, shelving, and legs of the furnishings. Do not choose matching suites of case goods (this is characteristic of passé salons), but instead pieces with finishes that are comparable in look and feel. The same is true of fabrics. Choose complementary tones, textures, and patterns that create a soothing elegant look.

- Display items in pairs and position them symmetrically. Create a balanced presentation of sofas, chairs, lamps, and accent pieces. This balanced and established presentation is calming and reassuring.

- Feature traditional details—skirts on the sofas and chairs, ornately carved woods, tailored draperies, crown molding, chandeliers, gilded picture frames, Oriental rugs, and timeless accents of bronze, gold, and silver.

- To keep the room from becoming stuffy, introduce elements of surprise and delight. Display an unusual piece of sculpture, use a box or trunk as a chairside table, or replace a sofa with a luxurious chaise. Lighten the mood with a free-form display of glass vases, crystal paperweights, or a vibrant pair of accent pillows. The possibilities are endless, but be careful. Too many unexpected details can detract from the room's classic style.

- Favor tailored details over fussy treatments when the designing draperies, upholstery, and pillows. Keep trims understated, pleats clean, and silhouettes simple.

19

INFORMAL SPACES

Comfortable should not only describe today's family room, but also the people living in it. If you long for a living room that is the heart of the home, where family and friends naturally gravitate to socialize, watch TV, or just hang out, detail can help. This informal living space, often called the family room, can be as inviting as a favorite armchair—familiar, nurturing, relaxed. To infuse these characteristics throughout your living space, a keen eye must be kept on all aspects of the room's design.

From the surfaces to the furnishings, practicality and comfort are key. Floors should encourage you to walk around barefoot but not demand that you take off your shoes. Sofas and chairs should accommodate a group of friends as well as a solitary nap on a Saturday afternoon. Accessories should be casually displayed and reflect your personal style. Finishes and fabrics should offer a play of color and texture and, perhaps most of all, not run and hide from frequent wear and an occasional spill. All and all, comfortable should not only describe today's family room but also the people living in it.

LEFT
Texture plays an important part in the casually styled living space. Here, a sisal rug, slipcovered armchair, and interior glass-paned door combine to create this room's relaxed ambience.

OPPOSITE
A loose pillow-back sofa, wicker chair, and glass-topped verde antique iron table unite unrelated forms and finishes. The lightly patterned dhurrie rug, broad-striped cotton upholstery fabric, and solid draperies help keep the look simple and uncluttered.

Variety is said to be the spice of life, and in a truly informal space, matching is limited. In this casual family room, a mixture of materials and forms combine to create the relaxed feel of the space. A leather armchair has a fabric-covered seat. An iron end table sits by one arm of the sofa while a wooden trunk rests by the other. Unmatching lamps perch on both pieces. An assortment of fabrics features a jumble of colors, textures, and patterns. Books and accessories appear casually set rather than purposefully placed.

LEFT
A rugged-stone fireplace, slate floors, and rough-hewn beams lend a natural, texture-rich feel to this inviting family room. A timeworn wooden trunk, a basket-based lamp, and a collection of Turkish oil jars further enhance the room's rustic atmosphere.

BELOW
Layering unrelated fabrics is a key part of detailing informally styled spaces. By simply placing a crumpled linen pillow against rich burgundy leather, this roll-armed sofa "feels" more at ease.

CREATING A COMFY AND CASUAL LOOK

If you desire a carefree family room where casual style and uncontrived details are perfectly at home, try the following:

- Select contrasting, unmatched elements for the room's furnishings. Wrought iron, painted pine, hammered copper, honed granite, and weathered oak are just the beginning of materials that combine to create a casual, down-to-earth style.

- Display collections of meaningful accessories and photographs in casually orchestrated, asymmetrical groups. They put your stamp of personality on the space and create points of interest.

- Take your cue from nature and feature texture-rich, natural materials throughout the room. Woven wicker, live plants, rough-hewn wood, pottery, sisal, and rugged stone, all add to a relaxed ambience.

- Create comfortable furniture groupings that accommodate gatherings of guests. Place sofas and chairs around a central coffee table and provide each with a nearby table on which to set drinks and snacks.

- Choose relaxed fabrics—textured chenille, soft cotton, brushed twill, suede. Accessorize with assorted pillows and consider using slipcovers to create a new look from season to season.

- Use unusual objects as furniture. Benches, stools, trunks, overturned baskets, and stacked suitcases create unique tables.

OPPOSITE
Mix-and-match fabrics, finishes, and materials give this living room its easy-going charm. An interplay of blue and white throughout binds the decorative elements together and makes the room feel serene and playful.

UPPER
This room's neutral color palette provides the perfect stage for its mixture of summertime accessories. Assorted pillows, candles, seashells, and pottery shape the seaside theme.

LOWER
Painted varied shades of blue and green, these old wooden ladders perform as unique accents while emphasizing the room's height.

GREAT ROOM

If you hunger for a living room that really cooks, consider the great room. The great room is the floor plan of choice for active families who enjoy spending a lot of time together. The recipe is simple. Take one part family room, add a kitchen and a dining room. Then stir in a measure of media room, entertainment room, and a pinch of home office. You'll dish up the most used and versatile space under roof.

Originally designed to replace a series of rarely used rooms with one open space, the great room has quickly become the floor plan of choice for active families. This multipurpose room not only makes more use of each square foot of space but also provides family members the opportunity to spend more time together while they perform unrelated activities like cooking, dining, watching TV, or just hanging out. However, with the great room's benefits come challenges. Homeowners may pack a circus of activities into the great room, but dislike the chaos and confusion that can result from the combined spaces. That is when smart design solutions come into play.

PAGE 26
Furniture, area rugs, and ceiling details divide this vast great room into intimate living, dining, and cooking areas. At the same time, warm buckskin colored walls and rich wooden floors help unite them.

ABOVE
This great room's open, airy space relies on dramatic ceiling detail, bold furniture groupings, and strong focal points. A built-in video screen and a framed oil painting define and delineate the areas of the space.

By definition, the great room is an open space comprising a social area, a kitchen, and a dining spot. The size and number of zones should depend on those who use the room. To create your ideal great room, consider how you and your family live.

- Do you love cooking and having others around you while you do?

- Do you enjoy throwing lavish dinner parties?

- Do you like hanging out with friends and family while watching movies on a large-screen TV?

Whatever your lifestyle, the components of your personalized space should reflect your needs and wants; a large kitchen, a small dining nook, a grand seating area, a built-in media center—the options are unlimited.

Once you have determined your great room's zones, the room's layout and design should be created to clearly delineate them from one another. At the same time, the space as a whole should appear aesthetically unified. This can be tricky. While separating a great room into individually defined zones makes it function well and feel more cozy, it can it weaken the cohesiveness of the space overall.

Designing well-integrated great rooms is a balancing act using both unifying and delineating details to create a cohesive look by flowing design elements directly from one space to the next. Even the largest great room's areas can be united by running a single flooring material, wall finish, or ceiling detail from one zone into the other.

On the other hand, you can break the entire room into more intimate spaces by creating delineating boundaries, using color, light, furniture arrangements, and surface materials. Structural details like varied ceiling heights, multiple floor levels, and partial walls often indicate a division of space or function. Frequently, architecture and the treatments of large surface areas are used to unite a great room's zones while strategically planned decorative details are employed to visually separate these same zones.

OPPOSITE
Here, eggplant-colored plaster anchors this great room's zones. The walls help define the living area by the fireplace and the kitchen behind the breakfast bar. Varied flooring treatments also signify different zones.

UPPER RIGHT
This colorful wall separates the kitchen from the nearby dining area while its large, interior "window" opens the cooking space to the dining zone.

LOWER RIGHT
This sinuous ceiling detail not only adds lively shape and structure to the room but also indicates a division of space and function.

DEFINING ZONES IN A GREAT ROOM

While uniting the areas of a great room can be as simple as flowing the same treatment throughout the entire space, delineating each zone from the other requires a carefully orchestrated strategy. Here are some simple and effective ways to indicate a division of space or function.

- Raise or lower parts of the ceiling and enlist varied ceiling details.

- Use different flooring materials or details in separate areas.

- Install partial walls to delineate zones.

- Vary colors and textures in each separate area.

- Use rugs to create the illusion of separate rooms within the great room.

- Arrange furniture groupings to shape boundaries. Backs of sofas, circles of chairs, tables, and chests can create natural spatial boundaries.

- Form a division between the cooking and living areas of the great room by installing a kitchen island or breakfast bar.

- Insert lighting that illuminates each zone with a different effect.

- Feature varied wood tones and cabinet finishes from zone to zone.

- Use single large paintings or tightly grouped art to create zone-defining focal points.

ABOVE
The breakfast bar's shiplap millwork reinforces the staggered, layered aesthetic seen throughout the room. Functionally, the bar provides casual dining seating and transition from the family room into the kitchen.

OPPOSITE
Continuity of materials unifies the areas of this great room's white oak millwork, parchment colored Venetian plaster, and softly-toned upholstery. Cantilevered glass-front cabinets as well as walls of varied heights help separate the living and cooking zones.

ENTERTAINMENT ROOM

If you live to be entertained, chances are your home reflects it. Today, media rooms, recreation rooms, game rooms, and high-tech family rooms have become must-have living spaces for many homeowners. By whatever name, the entertainment room frequently hosts any number of key elements: a large-screen TV, a complex audio/visual system, a game table or pool table, a bar or secondary kitchen space. That's a lot of activity to pack into one space. It's also a lot of unrelated features and furnishings to bring together.

To make this fun-loving room function well, hard-working detail is a must. It serves as a ringmaster, tying this circus of unrelated elements together. The first and most important step in creating an entertainment room is to establish its activities and the correlating furnishings and features for each. Prioritizing the importance of each activity will help determine primary and secondary focal points, shape furniture groupings, and steer statements of style. In a room where enjoyment is key, always keep comfort in mind.

PAGE 35
A brilliant violet wall draws your eye behind the kitchen counter. The black, white, and silver color palette makes this statement of color even more dynamic. The floor's graphic also creates a daring point of interest for the playful space.

OPPOSITE AND ABOVE
Matching rugs with fluid designs anchor and accentuate the pool table and sitting areas. A mono-chromatic brown creates an elegant dramatic backdrop for the brilliant blue underfoot. A pool table and a conversation area, focused on a large-screen video wall, compose the room's primary activity zones.

The entertainment room is created for casual get-togethers and should have lots of room to move around, multiple furniture groupings that encourage relaxed conversation, and activity areas that center around a pool table, bar, or TV. As with all rooms, it is important to establish desirable focal points in the entertainment room. These points guide visitors through the space, creating rhythm, points of interest, and weight. Without them, rooms appear unfinished, ungrounded, and uninspired.

Given the many prominent features entertainment rooms naturally have—game tables, media centers, numerous seating arrangements—they rarely lack focal points. Instead, the challenge is organizing these stimulating items, emphasizing some and downplaying others. The room's primary focal point is often obvious. It is the first feature or object that catches your attention when you enter the room: a bold fireplace, an oversized video screen, a large painting, or a dominant piece of furniture. If the prominent feature is desirable, enhance it further with detail. Add color and lighting and face furnishings toward it. If you want to downplay it, do just the opposite and choose another eye-catching object to emphasize.

Secondary focal points are also attention-grabbing but have less impact than the dominant primary focal point. You should accentuate these as well, but to a lesser degree. Remember, in most rooms, three major focal points are enough. If your eye responds to so many features that it never rests, you have created too many points of interest.

Who would have ever thought something called the "boob tube" would become the source of some of the most smartly conceived design ideas? Televisions have become mainstays in entertainment rooms, and integrating them into an interior's décor can be vexing. Two opposing, yet equally effective, approaches exist today: some homeowners choose to hide TVs away cleverly, while others choose to display them boldly. Whether deciding to hide or flaunt your television and exactly how to do it are best decided as early in the design process as when the architectural plans are being drawn. Working early and smart saves money and prevents the headaches that inevitably result from trying to work in technology after the fact.

ABOVE
This television descends from a ceiling panel, so it doesn't require wall space. Whether hidden or in full view, it is completely out of the way. The TV tilts when it drops to adjust the viewing angle.

RIGHT
Recessed into the wood-paneled wall of this handsome entertainment room, the TV's cabinetry is hidden with only the screen left visible. This eliminates any style-related conflict the appliance may have with the room's décor.

INCORPORATING TVS INTO A SPACE

If you choose to hide rather than flaunt your TV, here are a few ways to do it.

- Place the TV in a wall recess and cover it with art on a track, permitting it to slide out of the way for TV viewing.

- Create a "pop-up," or a television that rises on command from inside a piece of furniture such as a chest, console, or countertop. Today's thin profile televisions make hiding televisions easy.

- Drop the TV out of the ceiling. This approach requires expertise, because the viewing angle of a television perched high above a viewer's head must be perfectly tilted so the screen can be seen well.

If you would rather openly display your TV, try one of these ideas.

- Encase a thin-profile TV in a decorative frame and hang it like a piece of wall art. Ornate gilded frames can make even today's contemporary sets suitable for a traditional room.

- Display and disguise a TV at the same time. Purchase a DVD that scrolls beautiful works of art across the screen when the television is not in use.

- Install the TV in a wall niche to tone down its slick appearance and neutralize the TV cabinet's contemporary appearance.

- Incorporate a TV into existing or customized shelves; insetting the set helps disguise its bulk.

SPECIAL SPACES

There's no question that work and relaxation are part of living, so why not make a place for both of them in your living room? In today's open living areas, where space flows freely and activity often dominates the room, it is important to willfully incorporate special spaces that create a place to work or a spot to simply retreat and relax without distraction. This refuge may be a desk built into an alcove or a secretary that houses a computer and work surface, doubling as a display cabinet when closed. It may also be a corner outfitted with a small table, quiet lighting, and a chair and ottoman perfectly situated for solitude.

Special spaces don't necessarily require a lot of square footage and can be incorporated into a living room with just a bit of planning. The key: carve out an area that stylishly fits into, yet is somewhat removed from, the goings-on of the rest of the room. Your home may already have an architectural nook or recess to tuck your hideaway into; if not, use decorative details— shelves to screens and furnishings to finishes—to create one. You can incorporate a special refuge within your living room with just a little planning and a bit of ingenuity.

WORK SPACE

The home office, whether used for personal or professional purposes, has become a modern-day must-have. For many people, the office shares real estate with the main living area. Attention to detail is necessary for this arrangement to work well. Whether it's a center used solely for everyday paperwork or an all-out workstation, the space should be designed to accommodate the functional needs of the homeowner and blend seamlessly with the room's décor.

To create your own work area, provide the essentials: an ergonomic chair, abundant general and task lighting, storage space, a large work surface, and the necessary equipment and materials for the job. Select each of these components with the decorative theme of the living space in mind.

Design ample storage space into your home office to avoid intrusive clutter. When the work is finished, it should be tucked away allowing you to escape from thoughts of work, A secretary provides an ideal solution for living-space workstations. The cabinet doors and fold-up desk provide out-of-sight storage space for the muddle of work-related materials and opens and closes with ease.

When selecting your desk, choose the largest work surface possible without encroaching on the aesthetics of the room. Make certain it is solid and stable. Avoid eyestrain by shunning brightly colored or reflective work surfaces. Choose a chair that is comfortable and fits your frame. Dining chairs are not proper work chairs. Rollaway desk chairs are specifically designed for the work function and can be easily hidden away when the work is complete. The correct chair allows your feet to rest flat on the floor with knees angled at ninety degrees.

Create ways to hide or disguise the electric cords and cables that accompany today's workstations. Built-in channels and recesses are designed into many of today's home-office desks. If you favor an antique secretary or cabinet, drill an inconspicuous hole in the back of the piece so that cords can run behind it undetected.

PAGE 41
Stylishly incorporated into a contemporary living space, this library-office is framed by walls of shelves providing abundant display and storage space. A modern desk helps maintain the room's open, airy feel of the space, and is paired with an attractive leather desk chair that is ergonomically designed.

PAGES 42–43
This secretary is positioned beyond the center of the room and when opened, provides a comfortable place to work at the fold-down desk. When closed, its richly detailed design punctuates the room with timeless style. Directing the focus of the room's other furnishings away from the work area creates a sense of privacy where one works.

OPPOSITE
This work area is defined by architectural detail. A jog in a wall is enough to suggest the positioning of this small desk and chair. The window provides abundant daylight, while lamps provide plentiful task lighting.

LEFT
This secretary is both stylish and highly functional as a primary focal point. This sizable piece adds contemporary character and plentiful storage space.

SOLITUDE

Who doesn't enjoy a little time alone? Everybody needs private time to reflect, relax, or simply retreat. Given this, a truly livable living room features comfortable areas for both social and solitary activities. After all, with the vigorous lifestyles of today's families, it's vital that the living area of the home provides a refuge designed for a little downtime.

Creating a snug retreat requires a little space and a generous dose of detail. Some homes have spaces that are just inherently designed for a little quiet time. Sunlit window seats, intimate inglenooks, and concealed alcoves are among these. In other living rooms, however, one may need to ingeniously shape a getaway. Even if your living space doesn't naturally offer a quiet area removed from the rest of the room's activity, you can create one. All it takes is a comfortable seat, nice lighting, and a nearby table or ledge to place a candle, book, and beverage.

LEFT
Inspired by the Art and Crafts period, this modern-day inglenook forms a retreat blanketed in richly finished wood, patterned textiles, and warm lighting.

ABOVE
An adjustable lamp with soft light is an important part of creating a quiet refuge for reading.

CREATING A LIVING-ROOM RETREAT

Providing your living room with a quiet place to pause will add to its use and enjoyment. Consider the following ways to create your own refuge:

- Shape a spot for settling in with a great book by including a reading light. Whether it's a table lamp, floor lamp, or hinged lamp, position it so that it comes from over your left shoulder if you are right-handed and the opposite if your are left-handed. Situate the lamp so that the lower edge of its shade is at eye level. This will eliminate exposing your eyes to the bulb's glare.

- Locate a small table within reach of the chosen seating piece. Keep the table clear of unnecessary knickknacks so that a cup of tea and a book or magazine can be set down with ease. Keep coasters close at hand to avoid water rings on the tabletop.

- Position an ottoman at the foot of the reading chair. Mixed or matched with the style of the chair, an ottoman makes the space even more inviting and comfortable. In a tight spot, a nearby footstool or bench can be pulled into place, allowing you to put your feet up and relax.

- Place shelves, a woven basket, decorative box, or even a copper tub within arm's reach for storage of magazines, books, and a comfy lap blanket.

OPPOSITE
Perfectly positioned between a sunny window and a warm fireplace, this chair and ottoman shape a retreat for quiet time alone. Nearby shelves not only frame the cozy corner, but also offer a place to keep books and magazines. The small chairside table is ideally sized for holding a beverage or snack.

RIGHT
The sunny bank of windows illuminating this single chair, table, and lamp is conducive to reading and quiet contemplation. A small pillow provides extra comfort and support.

Once you have determined the type of living space that is best for you, it is time to physically stage the room. In your home, as in theater, this is accomplished by designing the set of the room—its floor, ceiling, walls. These structural elements define the space's dimensions, anchor its design, and perform as backdrops to the players—the furnishings and fixtures placed throughout. These surfaces also provide you with enormous opportunity to express your personal taste and style. When determining the treatment of your surfaces, look at each individually and judge both their practicality and their aesthetic appeal. Then consider the relationships that exist among them. This is very important. While each of the three surfaces has unique decorative and serviceable characteristics that are important to the way the room functions and feels, they must also work together to create the ambience and style you desire.

You may choose to have any or all of the surfaces play leading roles in your room's design, leaving supporting roles for the fixtures and furnishings. On the other hand, you may choose to create an understated backdrop that allows the amenities to dominate the scene. It all depends on your personal taste. Determine which direction you prefer before making any choices, and your job as a design director will be much easier.

As a general rule, people are most at ease with a set that takes nature's lead—a darker floor (earth), midtoned walls (vegetation), a light ceiling (sky). This approach is easily duplicated in the living room. You may, however, want something more dramatic. Why not shake things up a little? Just as theater is limited only by one's imagination, so are the design and detail you lavish upon your surfaces. While you keep an eye on practicality, let your originality flow to create a stylish room that is uniquely yours.

SURFACES

FLOORS

The influence a floor treatment has on the practical and aesthetic strength of a living room is enormous. This multitalented surface not only performs as the structural foundation of the room, it acts as the decorative foundation as well. Single-handedly, it can shape the personality of the room.

As a structural element, the floor is judged foremost on its durability. After all, is there another surface that takes more wear and tear than the floor of the busiest room in the home? When deciding on underfoot materials, weigh the practical advantages and disadvantages of the various choices available. Consider things like traffic patterns, exposure to sun and soiling, and the effect a flooring material has on sound in the room.

Once you have determined the viability of a specific surface treatment, take a thoughtful look at the aesthetic contributions it makes to the space. Simply by its square footage, a floor's appearance can make or break the room's decorative statement. With the amount of texture, color, and pattern a flooring material can deliver to a living room, its value as a design detail is all-powerful.

PAGE 50
Providing a dramatic backdrop for this large-living space, a geometric area rug, stacked-stone, and wood beams deliver pattern and texture that shape the refined yet rustic décor.

PAGE 53
A center circle and lines that radiate from the room's core are scored in this richly stained concrete floor. The design complements the ceiling treatment overhead.

OPPOSITE
This vividly toned, woven flat-weave rug relies on neutral furnishings and walls to balance its bold pattern and colors.

ABOVE
An understated round rug anchors a game area while a bold geometric rug defines a play area with its light-hearted tic-tac-toe pattern.

In sizable spaces like a living room, a detailed floor helps anchor the room and its décor. A variety of materials and treatments can provide an element of pattern, color, and texture to a floor; area rugs, carpets, and mats are the most popular and dynamic ways to impact the surface with character. From colorful kilims and dramatic dhurries to elegant Orientals and contemporary customs, rugs of different styles, shapes, and sizes can drive the living-room's design, define its zones, and unite furniture groupings placed on top of the rugs. In addition, rugs can provide underfoot comfort and soften the noise in a room with hard, unadorned stone or wood flooring.

USING RUGS IN THE LIVING ROOM

Rugs cover your floors with character and comfort. Here are some tips for choosing and incorporating rugs into your home.

- Choose statement-making rugs before furnishing a space. The task of selecting furniture and accessories that complement the colors and patterns of a rug is much easier than finding a rug that perfectly fits an existing décor.

- Protect area rugs from wear and tear by placing a pad beneath them. The proper pad depends upon the type of flooring surface beneath the rug; carpets require pads designed to keep a rug from bunching up while harder surfaces need nonslip pads that provide cushioning. The pad's dimensions should be slightly smaller than the rug's.

- To create an inexpensive custom-sized rug, cut a piece of carpet, sisal, or seagrass to the required dimension and have it bound with canvas or leather edging. Identical bound rugs used in a large great room can aid in creating continuity throughout the space.

- Choose patterned rugs to help disguise and minimize the stains and soiling common in areas of heavy traffic and use.

- For a one-of-a-kind look, create a floorcloth by painting a piece of canvas with a colorful design, then applying multiple coats of polyurethane for protection.

- Look beyond traditionally shaped rectangular rugs to help create interest and delineate seating areas. Round and square area rugs, customized shapes, and long runners can accommodate rooms or zones that are oddly proportioned.

OPPOSITE
Anchoring the living room
with subtle tones and an
intricate pattern, this rug
complements the solid
fabrics and finishes found
elsewhere in the room.

ABOVE
While large stone tiles cover
this home's floor, a sisal
rug is used to add softness
and define the main sitting
area. The rug's black
binding emphasizes the
separation of the hard and
soft surfaces.

When deciding on surface treatments for your living-room floor, analyze the
traffic patterns of the space and the sort of use each of the room's varied zones
will experience. Determine which parts will suffer the most wear and tear and
which will demand cushioning and softness for comfort. Hard surfaces like
stone, concrete, wood, and tile are resilient to heavy traffic and easier to
maintain than less permanent treatments like carpeting or area rugs. These less
durable materials are best used away from areas of intense foot traffic, where
they can deliver style, softness, and soundproofing to the space.

Whether you decide on travertine, oak, ceramic tile, or carpet, distinctive
flooring materials can bring a personalized look and unique style to your living
space. If a single flooring element is too overpowering, too expensive,
underwhelming, or lacking interest, integrate a second element into the design.
Stone tiles dissected with strips of wood, an island of textured carpet bordered
by marble, or free-form flagstone inset with colorful mosaics, all present a play
of powerful detail for your floor.

Consider the many options when selecting the best flooring materials, hard and soft, for your living space.

HARD FLOORING

Hard flooring materials provide a space permanence, durability, and distinctive character. The natural texture and color of hard flooring, as well as its pattern, help direct the style of the room.

STONE

Highly durable, stone in its many forms—granite, travertine, slate, marble—is a favorite of many homeowners. From rustic to refined, it is suitable for a range of décors. Because stone can be "hard" on the feet, area rugs are advisable to provide comfort underfoot and a soft place for young children to play and fall. Radiant heat helps remedy stone's coldness.

CONCRETE

Hard-wearing, concrete is particularly popular in contemporary settings. It can be textured, smooth, or rough, and easily accommodates radiant heat to warm its surface. Colorful stains, rich finishes, and imaginative scorings can transform this drab industrial material into floor art for your home.

TILE

Tile is a sturdy material made of ceramic, terra-cotta, or porcelain. It comes in unlimited colors, textures, patterns, and sizes. Tile is an affordable alternative to stone and has been successfully created to replicate it. With a reliable finish and seal, it is impervious to water, spills, and soiling. Porous tile should be sealed, as should its grout, to resist stains. In cold climates, radiant heat is recommended and a textured finish is best where tracked-in water can make smooth tile treacherously slick.

WOOD

Warmer and more yielding than stone and tile, wood softens sound and vibrations in a room. It is available in a range of types, sizes, and shapes—from strips to panels to planks. Wood can be richly stained, brilliantly varnished, and boldly painted. Hardwoods like oak and maple resist mars, dents, and scratches better than softer varieties. Laminates provide a low-maintenance option.

SOFT FLOORING

Soft flooring materials like carpet, rugs, and fibers are unsurpassed in softening the look, feel, and sound of a living room. They come in infinite colors, patterns, and textures which can drive the room's design direction while creating an intimate, warm ambience. What's more, they are easily and less expensively changed than their hard-surface counterparts, but generally will not last as long.

FITTED CARPETING

From shag to deep pile, wall-to-wall carpeting blankets a floor in luxurious comfort. It helps absorb sound and is warm and comfy. Depending on the type and style selected, it can show traffic patterns and require frequent vacuuming. Wool is the most durable, while nylon is the most popular. In large living rooms, if wall-to-wall carpeting appears monotonous, its unvaried expanse can be broken by placing patterned area rugs across its surface.

NATURAL FIBERS

Natural fibers lend a casual, relaxed ambience to a living space. Sisal and coir offer durable, stain-resistant options; while jute, also attractive, is softer but doesn't wear as well in high-traffic areas. Be cautious of loosely woven fibers; they can catch heels, making them inappropriate as runners or for placement in active areas.

RUGS

Rugs, from plush Orientals to flatly woven kilims, add a layer of character and color to a living-room floor. Unlike fitted carpeting, rugs can be taken with you when you move and can be easily changed out to alter the look and feel of the space. Change rugs throughout the year to create a seasonal look—rich Orientals in the winter, flat pale dhurries in the spring, natural jute in the summer, autumn-shaded kilims in the fall.

LEFT
This room features both hard and soft flooring treatments. Floating on a hardwood floor, this subtly-patterned area rug delineates a conversation area, while adding texture and comfort to the space.

CEILINGS

When it comes to dramatic detail in today's living spaces, things are looking up—literally. Floating high above the room, the ceiling has become the dynamic darling of architects and designers, who are infusing the surface with unique character and eye-catching design.

Once neglected and overlooked, living-room ceilings were doomed to be white and boring. Today, intricate framing, bold beamwork, vibrant color, and unique imagery are used to add charisma to a ceiling. Some of these treatments may be purely decorative, while others help define areas of the room below. In large living areas that incorporate social, dining, and kitchen spaces, the varied levels and decorations of the ceiling can strongly influence the feel and flow of the entire room. Even in smaller living rooms, ceiling detail can strongly affect one's perception of the room's overall volume. A darkened ceiling can make a room feel more cozy and intimate, while a lighter color can make the ceiling appear to recede upward.

Ceiling detail can also balance a living space. In a living room lacking overhead decoration, the space often appears bottom heavy: all of its personality is sunk within the lower half of the room. Ceiling detail balances a room with upward visual interest, offsetting the mass of the décor below.

ARCHITECTURAL DETAIL

While paint is the easiest way to add stylish detail to a ceiling, architecture is often the most dramatic. It requires forethought during the design and building process or a fair amount of imagination and effort during a ceiling overhaul. Architectural detail ranges from fairly simple to highly elaborate.

MOLDING

Perhaps the most basic architectural detail is molding. Whether applied to the ceiling or at the top of the wall, molding draws the eye up to add perceived height to the room. Using high-profile molding and painting it a contrasting color will amplify this effect.

BEAMS

Beams can also add bold character. Spaced far apart, they add statement-making style without strongly affecting the ceiling's perceived height. Placed closely together, they can actually cause the ceiling to appear lower. By varying the direction of beams in the same room, you can also define zones in the area below.

SCULPTING

Sculpted and multilevel ceiling details can help delineate the living-room area while adding interest, varied volume, and unique character to the room overall.

STRUCTURAL ELEMENTS

Do not overlook the structural components of a ceiling. Exposed elements like metal ductwork, wiring, and raw timbers can turn a ho-hum living room into a high-style urban or rustic retreat.

Whatever choice you make, keep in mind that a room featuring boldly designed ceilings should be balanced with strong yet limited detail elsewhere in the room. Too many powerfully visual features can dilute the impact of each.

PAGE 61
This modern coffered ceiling visually lowers a lofty ceiling to make the room feel more comfortable. Its geometric grid is stylishly mimicked in a large group of framed art pieces.

PAGE 62
This European-flavored great room features two planes of beamwork. The upper-level treatment dresses the ceiling's actual surface while a series of large crossed beams drops the visual height of the room to make the space less cavernous.

PAGE 63
Large beams frame a rectangular "canvas" that boasts a rich painting in shades of ivory and taupe. The muted colors and indistinct design keep the detail from overwhelming the space.

ABOVE
Rounded, free-form ceiling structures add interest to this multi-zoned space, adding interest to the large space while helping to define its areas. Recessed lighting accentuates the islands of ceiling detail.

RIGHT
Accentuating this ceiling's unique shape and the room's Old World styling, a hand-painted celestial design features constellations the zodiac signs.

CREATING A DETAILED CEILING

If your ceiling is ho-hum, consider the many ways available to add character and space-altering detail to this overhead surface.

- If a room feels overwhelmingly large and uncomfortable due to a high ceiling, lower the surface perceptually by painting it a color or adding pattern to its surface. Flow the same treatment from the ceiling onto the walls to make the ceiling seem even lower.

- If a ceiling feels too low, paint it a light shade and frame it in a wide painted or paper border. The border will make the ceiling surface look smaller and loftier.

- To make a room cozier, paint the ceiling the same color as the walls. This mitigates the defining edges between the two surfaces, creating a blanket of color that embraces the overall space.

- Rather than painting the ceiling white in a room with colorful walls, paint the ceiling the same color lightened by seventy-five percent. The ceiling will be light but not white. This creates a more soothing and stylish transition from the walls to the ceiling.

- Emphasize a living room's decorative theme with hand-painted ceiling images or stenciled patterns. From faux architectural features to imitation clouds overhead, they will draw the eye upward and add drama and detail, making the space truly unique.

- If your ceiling has surface flaws, use wall-paper, fabric, or faux finishes on the ceiling to disguise them. Avoid covering blemishes with glossy paint as its reflective finish will accentuate them.

- Use fixtures that cast light upward, such as open-topped sconces, to throw intriguing shadows and a play of light on the ceiling's surface. Shine light upward through potted plants to provide instant patterns overhead.

OPPOSITE
Illumination and level changes are two dramatic ways to dress high-style ceilings. This spacious great room incorporates both and uses set-in lighting to stress the jagged, multilevel ceiling detail.

ABOVE
Consider the impact exposed structural elements can add to your space. This contemporary loft living area capitalizes on a grid of metal ductwork to emphasize its ceiling's height and the room's high-tech décor.

WALLS

Walls not only shape the boundaries and size of a living room, they also shape its personality. What character do your walls bring to your living area? To answer this question, picture your living room empty, with only the shell of the space remaining. Without its furnishings and fixtures, does your living room still have the ambience you want? If not, you may have anemic walls. It might be time to give them a healthy dose of decorative detail. There are many ways to do this; the simplest and least costly is color.

The color and texture of its walls can define the personality of your room. Painting a room a distinctive color instantly affects its mood as well as the way it feel. Depending on the color and tone selected, colored walls can make a space seem warmer or cooler, larger or smaller, vivacious or restrained. They can also unite the space visually.

Texture and pattern can also perform powerfully when applied to walls. Small patterns add character without imposing on the room, while large patterns accentuate a decorative theme and introduce dramatic dimension to the space. Large patterns should be used judiciously so they don't over-whelm the space. Architectural details like moldings, niches, and wainscoting can enliven flat featureless walls. Keep in mind that any vertical surface that shapes the room is part of its walls. Freestanding shelves, half-walls and railings, fireplaces, screens, and even windows and doors act as parts of a room's walls as they define and detail this horizontal surface. These features add interest to walls that might otherwise appear drab. They break them up and create pockets of intrigue. However, without careful placement, they can make the room appear scattered, as its walls become peppered with unrelated features and finishes.

INTEGRATION

In many living rooms, a number of dissimilar elements comprise much of the room's walls—media centers, fireplaces, display shelves, windows, doorways, architectural ledges, niches. With this multitude of unrelated features, the task of incorporating them into a beautifully decorated room can be challenging. The following can help:

COLOR

Visually bind the room together by finishing the walls in a single color or material that surrounds and encases the many features.

MATERIAL

Create continuity in the room by introducing the same material on multiple features. For instance, if you have an entertainment center crafted from oak, use this same wood to create a broad mantel over the fireplace, fashion the room's doors, and even carry it into one or two pieces of furniture. This links the disparate elements, giving the room flow. Be cautious to not overdo it, though; too much of the same material can turn a room from beautiful to bland.

MOTIF

Relate dissimilar wall-based elements by repeating the same shape or motif in various materials—square concrete blocks on a fireplace, square wooden panels on built-in cabinetry doors, square marble tiles to frame a niche. Again, avoid overdoing it. Pick just a few places to apply the motif; too much of the same detail can appear trite and overworked.

PAGE 69
A wall "floats" between floor and ceiling, screening one space from the next while allowing light and air to flow all around it.

LEFT
Free-formed wood, metal, and glass shape and unite the façades of the media center, fireplace, and partial walls. In addition, a golden-toned wood links fixtures throughout the space.

The contrast between solid and empty space is a powerful tool that can be used to bring remarkable detail to your walls. By breaking or punctuating the wall's surface with openings, you add dimension to the room. Windows are a wonderful example of introducing openness to a wall's surface adding interest and character.

To apply this same idea in other ways, consider the options. A simple screen raised on legs creates a barrier yet allows light and ambience to flow from the areas it separates. The same effect can be created by either raising an interior wall off the floor or by installing a partial wall that doesn't reach the ceiling. Interior walls can also be perforated so one part of the room can be viewed from another. Open shelving and niches as well as see-through fireplaces allow space and interior views to flow from area to area while they break and enhance the solid planes of the living-room walls.

LEFT
This striking room features open spaces where one would expect solid surfaces. The fireplace is open on three sides, allowing a view from one side to another, while a large niche opens a concrete-block wall to both spaces. Low-level cabinetry outlines one side of the room without closing it off from a neighboring area.

FIREPLACES

In today's home, the fireplace is one of the most loved and significant design elements. As a dramatic and comforting focal point, a fireplace can single-handedly define the character and personality of a room. We arrange room settings around it and display favorite objects near it. We gather around it with friends and family.

If you are designing or updating your fireplace, take inspiration from the period, style, and natural setting of your home. An older Victorian parlor and a contemporary loft merit entirely different fireplaces. One is likely to feature an ornately carved façade embellished with marble, while the other is left stark and unencumbered by distracting detail. Similarly, a home's site can provide direction. Mountain homes, for example, are often surrounded by rugged stone and raw timber; these can be incorporated into the chimney or mantel of a fireplace, tying it and the entire living room to the home's natural surroundings. A desert dwelling's flagstone hearth or a country cottage's stacked-rock chimney represent other site-inspired fireplace designs.

A newly constructed or renovated living room provides a blank slate for original design. For many homeowners, however, an existing lackluster fireplace presents a challenge. In this case, a simple facelift may be all that is needed to bring new character to the feature and the surrounding living room. Sometimes a new coat of paint or a new fire screen may be enough. Other times, the surface and structural application of anything from weathered brick to cultured stone, reclaimed metal to hand-formed tiles, can sufficiently enhance the feature. Other material options include timeworn timbers, faux painting, exotic woods, and even glass. The possibilities are limited only by your imagination.

ABOVE
Iron screens and tools can bring ornate or simple style to a fireplace. Placed on a rugged sofa table, a pair of iron accessories mimics a handwrought screen that dresses the front of this stone fireplace.

OPPOSITE
Performing as the focal point of a traveler's family room, this architecturally detailed fireplace ideally complements the room's eclectic collection of worldly finds.

OPPOSITE
This fireplace doesn't need
a mantel; its character is
underscored by stylish mini-
malism—from the
stainless-steel-framed
box, to the concrete
chimney and hearth. Its
asymmetrical position
on the wall underscores
its unique style.

ABOVE
A stone-clad fireplace
stylishly divides this large
living space into an active
family room and a quiet sitting space. Each zone can
be seen through and
around the feature.
Mimicking the room's wide
crown molding, a broad
white mantel links the
fireplace to the décor of
both areas and accentuates
the fireplace's
impressive width.

MANTEL

Of the fireplace's components, the mantel is the most direct link to the style and scale of the surrounding room. Massive and broad-shouldered, it can add weight and dimension to a firebox lacking size or proper proportions. Refined, it can make a subtle statement of style. An eclectic or contemporary setting may favor an asymmetrically placed mantel, while a traditional décor demands a symmetrically positioned mantel that provides predictable balance. Furthermore, a minimalist interior may be best served featuring no mantel at all, leaving a simple fireplace opening to emphasize the room's austerity.

HEARTH

The hearth, or floor in front of the fireplace, openly invites creative detail. A slab of stone, recycled bricks, brilliant tiles, or even glass blocks can protect the floor from flying sparks and burning embers. At the same time, they can add unique character to the room. A hearth also can be raised, offering a seat-height ledge for stacking logs, tools, and accessories.

BACKDROP

The fireplace's backdrop—the adjoining walls of the room—support the fireplace structurally and decoratively. Bold color, patterned paper, or a trompe l'oeil treatment can create a distinctive look. Floor-to-ceiling mirrors, windows, or bookcases that flank the fireplace emphasize its character and provide additional dimension to the wall. Brilliant spotlights or shaded sconces reinforce the style of the room while highlighting the fireplace and its accessories. The key is to think beyond the fireplace itself and incorporate detail into the surfaces encompassing it.

ACCESSORIES

Accessories are the crowning touch to the fireplace. Look first to the functional tools for interest. If you must have them, they might as well be stylish. Today's andirons, stokers, and screens have become works of art, incorporating everything from handwrought iron and pewter, to glass and stone. Be careful to choose stylistically appropriate pieces that complement rather than clash with the fireplace design and the room's décor. The same holds true of other accents like eye-catching fireboards and bins of copper, iron, or wood for storing logs and kindling.

ABOVE
A simple corner screen accentuates the blocky form of this fireplace and creates a two-sided firebox opening.

OPPOSITE
So that it doesn't compete with the outdoor views that frame it, this shelf-sided fireplace is thoughtfully designed using linear architecture and understated, minimally patterned materials.

DECORATING AN OFF-SEASON FIREBOX

Minus a roaring fire and smoldering embers, an off-season firebox often looks gloomy. By adding a flavorful detail or two, you can bring it back to life.

- Stack white-barked logs (birch or aspen) and bundles of kindling to fill a vacant box with interest and texture.

- Block the fireplace opening with a distinctive screen. Use ornate metal panels, panes of etched glass, or even old hinged shutters to elevate the fireplace's personality.

- Place potted flowering plants and lacy ferns inside the box. If low light exists, use silk plants to create the look of a flourishing flowerbox.

- Display a single vase, platter, tray, or basket within the opening to create a solitary focal point secondary to the fireplace itself.

- Position a collection of randomly sized pillar candles inside the box. Lighted, they create a relaxing ambience on a balmy summer night. When using several candles, make certain the flue is open for the heat and smoke to escape.

- Use a decorative antique fire grate to hold the burning wood of winter's fires. During the year's warmer months, fill it with pinecones in lieu of firewood to create a relaxed natural look.

- Incorporate uniquely designed andirons. Distinctively sculpted, they look like stylish sentries guarding the firebox opening.

- Cover the space with an imaginatively painted fireboard. Like a colorful painting, a fireboard can provide an image of a basket of blooming flowers or a sleeping pet perched on the hearth.

SHELVES

Multitalented and hardworking, shelves perform dynamic features in the living room. Freestanding shelves can divide a room while allowing the separate areas to stay open to one another. Built-in shelves can be inset into empty corners, niches, and recesses and used to frame a window or fireplace, adding depth and drama to the wall. Of course, simple platform shelf can run above a door or span an entire wall to provide abundant storage and display space.

When integrating shelves into your décor, ask a few simple questions to help you choose the right version for your living room.

- Do you need shelving to help with storage or for display?

This can influence the amount of shelving you install. Keep in mind that while books, decorative boxes, and cherished collections may be attractively stored and shown on shelves, tattered piles of magazines and everyday household items are best left behind closed doors.

- Do you want to employ shelving that doubles as a room divider?

If so, keep in mind that light should have plenty of room to pass through open shelves; objects placed on the shelves should not be crowded or bunched together.

- Can shelves add character and purpose to your room's empty spaces?

Here, display outweighs storage as a priority. If you want to use shelves to fill and add purpose to unused space in the room, consider empty corners, underutilized niches and recesses, or space above and around the doors and windows. Remember, shelves can be easily customized to fulfill the needs and wants you have for your personalized living space.

ABOVE
This narrow built-in cabinet was created to perform as a shelf, displaying black-and-white photography.

OPPOSITE
These custom-built shelves separate the living room from a colorful foyer. Sparkling glass vases form a bold display on the shelves without blocking the view and light that flows through them.

ABOVE
A number of wall openings, grouped together for impact, was specifically designed and lighted to display and protect these unique pieces.

OPPOSITE
When integrated during the construction or renovation of a room, shelves become a striking architectural element. This plastered grid of open boxes forms a wall of display shelves. Strong backlighting accentuates the outstanding feature.

If you are building or renovating a wall in your living room, why not personalize it with custom shelves or nooks? They provide wonderful places to display your treasured collectibles while creating intriguing focal points in the room. Depending on how you position these insets into the wall's surface, you can create an eye-catching grid or a rhythmic pattern of openings that contributes strongly to the room's décor. And, unlike broad tabletops and accessible mantels, each opening provides a safe out-of-the-way place to store and display cherished pieces that can be enjoyed while remaining relatively safe from the room's activity.

DESIGNING SHELVES AND WALL NICHES

While shelves add powerful detail to the walls of a living room, they themselves invite spectacular detail in a number of forms. If you have shelves or plan to install them, there are a number of ways to increase their impact on your space's styles.

- Use color to draw the eye into a shelf's opening and to tie it to the room's décor. By painting, faux-finishing, or papering the wall behind your shelves, you stress the shelves' importance as a focal point and create a bold backdrop for the items displayed. If you are positioning a specific collection of items on your shelves that you would like dramatized, use a contrasting hue on the wall behind them to make the pieces stand out and give them more punch.

- Incorporate lighting to accentuate the shelves and the items positioned on them. There are many options available. Single spots can be mounted in each opening, as can ropes of tiny lights that run along the underside of shelves. Small accent lamps can be displayed and illuminated on the shelves or small sconces can be mounted on the sides of the wall behind them. Whatever method you choose to illuminate your shelves, keep objects directly below lights dust-free; bright light exaggerates dust.

- Cover the wall behind shelves with a mirror. This creates the impression of open shelving with a room beyond it. It also draws light into dark corners and alcoves where shelves may be placed.

- Use glass shelves to keep the space open and airy. When using glass shelves, only a single light source placed above the shelves is needed to illuminate the entire feature from top to bottom, unless the light is obstructed by a large item or group of books. If you dislike dusting, don't use glass shelves. They show dust more than opaque materials like wood or metal.

- Use rounded or bullnosed edges on shelves to soften their look and to make them safer around young children.

OPPOSITE
Built-in shelves provide a
place for books and family
photos while creating a
backdrop for this relaxed
reading area. The flowing
horizontal lines add to the
simple, stylish design.

ABOVE
Twin sets of shelves,
symmetrically positioned to
balance this room, are
backed with burnt orange.
The color contrasts with the
brown walls and is illuminated by rope lighting, drawing
the eye to the shelves and
their displays.

Niches not only provide an out-of-the-way place to display your treasures, they create focal points and architectural interest to a room. When incorporating shelf-like niches into a wall, consider the following:

- Take inventory of each piece you want to house in the niches. Measure each item and customize the size of the opening in which the item will be placed. Provide enough space around each piece so that it doesn't appear jammed or crowded in the nook.

- Include built-in lighting to illuminate your collectibles and displays. The lighting will also accentuate the openings, giving them architectural significance and strength as dazzling focal points in your room.

- Position niches in groups, much like you would a gathering of similar pieces of art. This avoids a haphazard appearance and creates a unified focal point encompassing all of the openings. Don't be afraid to combine openings of different sizes and shapes, as long as they work together to create a single statement on the wall.

To the uninspired, a room's space is defined by its square footage: a small living room is small, a large one is large. It's simply a matter of fact. After all, a room's physical dimensions are shaped by its walls, floor, and ceiling. In a well-designed room, space is not tallied by a measuring tape alone. Instead, space becomes a less tangible element that's gauged by perception—the way the room feels beyond its computed square footage.

What impression does your living-room space present? Does the room feel large or cozy, small or cavernous, inviting or aloof? The truth is that few of us are blessed with the perfectly sized or shaped living room. The ideal room, as proven by the Greeks when they built the Parthenon, features a length that is 1.618 times longer that its width. This formula provides the most comforting and harmonious space perceptually. However, do not worry if your living room doesn't measure up to this calculation. With a generous dose of detail, you can alter the way your space feels and is perceived. There are a number of design elements that can help you do this, including scale, lighting, color, and texture.

Scale refers to the proportion of an object and how it relates to the space in which it is placed. We have all been in a room where a monstrous coffee table overwhelms a sitting area or an antique chair passed down through generations is just too tiny when positioned below lofty ceilings. The goal in creating a spatially pleasing room is to select items and details that are ideally scaled to help shape the atmosphere you desire.

Lighting can also affect the way you perceive a room's area. Light expands space and, when strategically orchestrated, can seemingly make a small area grow. Less light makes a too-large room seem more cozy and comforting. Light also helps direct movement and sight within a space.

Color and texture influence our perception of the mood of a space. A room painted dark brown will feel more cozy and compact than the same room painted a light beige. Similarly, rough grasscloth wall covering will constrict a room's space more than a high-gloss paint or finish.

Whatever spatial challenges your room presents and whichever of these tools you employ to address them, you can outwit the tape measure and shape a space that is perfect for you.

SCALE

Determining the proper proportion and scale in the living room is as important as choosing the perfect colors and materials, yet proper scale is often overlooked. We have all been in homes where the furnishings and features are the wrong size for the rooms. You don't want to make this mistake. Bringing home a new sofa that barely fits through the door and swallows up your living room can be enough of a problem. Yet, if you force your room to accommodate the sofa, its bulk will likely upset the balance and harmony of the space. This is a sure sign that the sofa's scale is inappropriate for the room. The same can be said of objects that are proportionately undersized. Scattered throughout your living room, they can disrupt the space, making it feel jumbled and disjointed. It's not that the sofa and objects are sized badly; it's just that they don't fit the room. They simply feel wrong; and that's how scale is assessed. Judging the scale of an object is based on a gut feeling about how it relates to the space, its fit, and its appropriateness. You will know when it feels right and when it feels wrong.

Before adjusting the scale of your living room, you need to evaluate the room's spatial characteristics. Are the ceilings uncomfortably high or low? Is the area small and confined or large and sprawling? Are the architectural features overwhelmingly bold or weakly understated? Any spatial quality of your living room that detracts from its ambience can benefit from well-scaled detail to help establish balance throughout the room.

The desirability of a room's size is judged by human scale: what the average-sized person finds most comforting. This relates to the room's volume, which is determined by the span of its space as well as the height of its ceiling. If a room is too small, it feels confining; too large, and it can be disconcerting. A room's dimensions affect us strongly.

For most of us, ceiling height is critical in establishing a room's comfort level. Of course, not all living rooms are created equal. Some feature low ceilings that can crowd and crunch us while others boast lofty ceilings that leave us lost and disoriented. Proper scale and in detail can bring these to a level that feels comfortable and appropriate.

LOW CEILINGS

If your room suffers from low ceilings, elevate its ambience with a mixture of tall and short design elements. For instance, tall doors, windows, and cabinetry that reach toward the ceiling will stretch the height of the walls, making the ceiling seem higher. These should be balanced with lower-profile furnishings in the room's center, leaving the room open and airy. A tall lamp or floral arrangement can help break up a clustering of shorter furnishings that are positioned in the middle of the room.

HIGH CEILINGS

If your room has high, soaring ceilings, choose tall furnishings whose scale matches the room's lofty volume. Avoid squatty tables and low-profile sofas and accents. Opt for pieces with elongated statures like high-back chairs and tall armories. Choose towering plants, lamps, and accessories to balance the ceiling's height. Position art high on the wall to fill the extended surface. Use darker colors and elaborate detail on the ceiling to bring it downward visually.

PAGE 87
Organized "clusters" of accessories and large single pieces of art and furniture make this space feel open and roomy. The white walls and ceiling add visual space as well as drama when paired with glossy, dark wood floors and an open staircase.

PAGE 89
Like color, size is inherent in every detail. Enormous paintings, large architectural cutouts, and a grouping of oversized chairs are ideally scaled to fit this capacious room.

OPPOSITE
While this room is short in stature, it is broad in area. Here, floor-to-ceiling doors and windows and a tall floor lamp add visual height to the room. Large-scale furnishings fill the space in proper proportion.

LEFT
Tall furnishings provide the appropriate scale for this room's high, lofty ceilings. A very tall floor lamp flanked by two high-back armchairs help balance this room's soaring ceiling. Even the arrangement of branches reaching skyward adds to the voluminous space.

LARGE SPACES

While most people consider large living rooms a luxury, these spaces present unique challenges. Not the least of these challenges is the cavernous and cold feeling a vast room can create. To remedy this problem, provide large rooms with large-scale detail to infuse size-appropriate character and personality into their space. This detail should be measured in mass, not quantity of pieces. The scale of furnishings and fixtures is more important to a room's design than the quantity of pieces. In fact, loading a room of any size with an excessive number of items just causes chaos and clutter that can only be reformed with strict organization. Simply put, large rooms require large statements of detail. This translates into sizable furnishings, accessories, accents, and artwork. The scale of each should be measured against the other objects as well as the volume of the room. For instance, a large sofa is best accompanied by a similarly scaled cocktail table, side chairs, and end tables. Each complements the others and balances the room as well. If you choose to feature smaller items in a large living room, place them in groups. Their combined mass can fool the eye into seeing a single larger design statement rather than a scattering of smaller ones.

RIGHT
Oversized furnishings are positioned in weighty horizontal groupings to balance the open area of this large living space. A high-hung painting, a tall potted plant, and soaring windows provide vertical dimension to fit and fill the room.

SMALL SPACES

When space is short, you have to keep a keen eye on detail. Every element in a room can add or detract from the limited area available. Fortunately, while small living rooms have less square footage, less storage, and less elbow room, they often inspire more ingenious design solutions and treatments. Among these is the use of scale. Properly applied, it can actually create the illusion of more space.

In general, small living spaces require small-scale furniture and features. They help balance the room so that it is not swallowed up by oversized pieces. You want to be especially careful with furnishings like sofas and cocktail tables that can appear moderately proportioned until they are placed in a small room, where they seem to grow to twice their size. To avoid this unpleasant revelation, be prepared with a full set of measurements of your living room when you go shopping and carry a tape measure to check the size of any piece you consider purchasing. What looks small in a showroom might overwhelm your bungalow's living space.

While small-scale pieces are well suited for small rooms, don't use them in excess. Too many pieces of any dimension can clutter a small room, seemingly shrinking its space dramatically. In fact, if you limit the number of furnishings in a small room, a large-scale item can be successfully incorporated. Because fewer pieces fill the area, the large piece won't seem crowded and its size can actually fool the eye into believing the room reflects the same proportion. To enlist this strategy, it is very important to keep the room free from clutter and excessive detail.

OPPOSITE
This large-scale mirror fills the corner of a small living space, reflecting light throughout the room. Nearby, a large armchair features an open frame that neutralizes its size by allowing space to flow around it. Both features expand the room visually.

USING SCALE TO UPSIZE A SMALL ROOM

There are some creative ways to use scale to make the most out of a modestly sized living room. They include:

- Incorporate reflective surfaces such as mirrors, glossy paint, shiny marble, or lacquered wood into the room. As light bounces off a shiny finish, the room visually expands.

- Group a collection of small items into a single large focal point rather than strewing them individually across the room. This applies to multiple pieces of framed art, pillows on a sofa, and cherished tabletop objects. Orderly display consumes less visual space in a room.

- Create areas of open space and light around individual pieces. Even large pieces of furniture with open legs and arms, glass tops, and raised platforms allow light to flow through them, opening the space visually.

- When introducing area rugs into your modestly sized room, choose a single large-scale rug rather than a number of smaller pieces. Numerous rugs make the room look busy while a single large rug will visually extend the room's area.

- Avoid large multicolored patterns in small rooms as they deplete visual space. Monochromatic patterns of any size are best suited for tight areas.

- Choose blinds rather than billowy draperies to dress windows. They lie flat against the wall taking less space, actual and visual, in the room.

LIGHT

How enlightened is your living room? If it isn't aglow with well-designed lighting, its decorative strength is likely in the dark. Like no other design element, light defines space and grants it character. Good lighting is essential in creating a dynamic, highly functional living space. With the flip of a switch, light can make a room appear larger or smaller causing the same space to appear warmer and welcoming or cooler and reserved.

In the living room, as in other areas of the home, light performs both practical and decorative functions. By recognizing these functions, the type of light that achieves them, and the many ways to orchestrate light throughout your living space, you can wash your living room in high-voltage style. By merging natural, ambient, task, and accent lighting into your living room, you'll have a space that not only works well but is brimming with personality.

The simplest source of illumination is natural light. Harnessed indoors, sunlight can wash a living room with everchanging character throughout the daylight hours. The amount of natural light enjoyed by a room is restricted by the dimension and direction of the windows. However, you can make the most of the light coming in by keeping the windows unencumbered by heavy dressings and amplifying the light with reflective surfaces.

Ambient, or general, lighting provides an overall level of light in the room and can be created by a number of manmade sources, including overhead fixtures, torchères, wall sconces, pendant fixtures, and table lamps. Combining any number of these affords a stylish way to fill the room with the basic illumination it needs to be functional. Task lighting tackles special illumination needs in areas where specific activities like reading, writing, cross-stitching, and playing board games take place. Reading lamps and focused pendants serve these work-oriented requirements. Finally, accent lighting is predominantly decorative and is used to shape the ambience of the space by highlighting notable architecture, art, and special features in the room.

To understand good lighting, you must recognize its purpose. It does much more than simply eliminate darkness and prevent you from tripping over the ottoman. It highlights architectural and design details, facilitates comfortable movement through the living room, brightens work areas, and affects the view indoors and out. Simply put, it enhances the aesthetic and functional qualities of the room.

Creating well-designed lighting can be compared to executing a fine oil painting. The living room is the canvas, and the light, like richly colored paints, is applied in layers that combine to create a single statement. No one layer of light, or paint for that matter, should detract from the finished work. Instead, each should complement the other.

PAGE 97
This room benefits from a wide expanse of windows. Draperies are minimal and are closed only when privacy is needed.

RIGHT
This space's architecture is subtly backlit, while dramatic accent lights accentuate a large oil paintings. Ceiling spots provide general lighting while illuminated cylinders add personality.

LAYERING LIGHT

There are many kinds of illumination that can be layered to create a well-lighted space. To execute fine lighting design in your living room, include:

- Lights used to accentuate the living room's structural features, including the beams, niches, columns, coves, and other notable architectural elements.

- Ornamental fixtures like chandeliers and sconces that dress up the room like jewelry, sparkling with eye-catching light without fully illuminating the space.

- Lighting fixtures that highlight sculptures, paintings, gallery walls, displays of collectibles, and other statements of art.

- Guiding lights that help you move through the space, such as lights that brighten paths, steps, and level transitions in a great room.

- Work-oriented lighting that enables you to read, sew, write, or perform other activities requiring strong, focused light.

- Accent lights that focus on and flatter decorative details and furnishings in the room, including an armoire, draperies, sofas, tables, or even interior plants.

- Outdoor lighting that enhances the view both inside and outside of the windows. By placing exterior lighting close to the house, you create a focal point beyond the living room, mitigating the reflection of interior lights on the glass. Lights positioned farther into the yard can highlight landscape features like pools, statues, gazebos, and trees; and lure the eye outward, visually expanding the space of your living room.

REFLECTIVE SURFACES

Surfaces such as mirrors, glossy paint, and shiny metals can help brighten your living room by attracting light and reflecting it back into the space. They can make large, statements on the floor, walls, and ceiling and create eye-catching spots of sparkle as they dance on the room's accents and accessories.

Mirrors perform magic in the living room. Effortlessly, they take the available light in the room and double its space-stretching impact by bouncing it back into the living area. At the same time, mirrors multiply the room's decorative power by doubling the image of each item and detail in its view. This successful sleight of hand does not occur without some planning, however. There are a number of ways to position and place mirrors to enhance their reflective powers.

Consider the image a mirror returns. It should be one you enjoy. For example, placing a mirror opposite a window that frames a wonderful view provides the vista twice over. Similarly, placing a mirror directly behind a table of cherished collectibles doubles the treasures' impact. Position a framed mirror on top of a chest or on the floor and lean it against the wall at a slight angle. You'll not only see the reflection of the space in front of the mirror but also the ceiling detail above it.

Mirrors can create architectural imagery as well. Framing a fireplace with a floor-to-ceiling mirror creates the impression that the fireplace divides two rooms—the one you are in and the one the mirror's reflection creates. Positioning a mirror inside an alcove, a window frame, or a doorway creates the illusion that the room continues through the opening. This trickery only works if the mirror's edges disappear into the perimeter of the architectural feature.

At its most powerful, a mirror that seamlessly covers an entire wall can make it vanish, seemingly doubling the size of the room.

ABOVE
A mirrored chest not only provides storage but also creates a stunning decorative statement that reflects the room's décor and visually consumes minimal space.

OPPOSITE
This tall, simply framed mirror calls attention to its surroundings. It is staged on the table to reflect and double the accessories' impact.

Of course, mirrors aren't the only reflective surfaces. A myriad of decorative surfaces are available today that can heighten the light level in your living space, including:

- Acrylics accessory
- Burnished leather
- Glass tabletops
- Glazed ceramics
- Glossy oil paintings
- High-sheen paint
- Metal accent pieces
- Metallic and shiny wallpaper
- Polished wood
- Satin fabrics
- Shiny stone

RIGHT
A dark-wood ceiling requires the help of shine and sparkle to lighten the room's overall interior. Acrylic lamps, a silky upholstered sofa, a polished stone tabletop, and a dramatic series of large framed mirrors reflect light and open this room to refreshing design.

OPPOSITE UPPER RIGHT
The impact of a single vase sparsely filled with flowers is increased by posing a mirror behind it.

OPPOSITE LOWER RIGHT
This ornately framed mirror augments an opulent décor while drawing in light and imagery.

COLOR

In the world of detail, color reigns supreme. While many elements contribute to the look and feel of a living space, color is one of the most important. Its power to bring life to your interior is absolute. Fortunately, you control the colors you introduce into the room: the paint and finishes on the walls and ceiling, the treatments on the floors, the furnishings and fixtures you place throughout. Each of these wears color that affects the ambience of the space. While color choice is a very personal matter, we all have our favorites. Look beyond your general likes and dislikes, and recognize the influence different colors have on a room. Use your space as a guide. Do you have any spatial flaws or limitations that color can help remedy? Is the room too large, or the ceilings too low, or the windows too few?

The right color can help hide or minimize these shortcomings. Light colors can make a room look larger. When placed on the walls and ceiling, they expand the interior space by reflecting light into the room. They also amplify the restricted natural light that a room may receive through limited or undersized windows. Conversely, darker, deeper tones advance on the space, drawing the room inward and making it seem smaller and cozier. While color reshapes the perceived dimensions of a room, it also affects the mood. Few other design elements bring such an immediate change to a space.

While color can help you shape the perception of your room to a more desirable size, it can also affect the ambience. What mood do you want for your living room; do you want it to feel stimulating or soothing, intimate or exhilarating? Your decision can help influence your color choices.

Generally, cool tones of blue, green, gray, and icy white make a room calming and serene. While these cool shades are great space makers when applied to walls—making them recede, they can also make a room feel cold. Warmer shades of red, yellow, orange, and beigy white make a room feel cozier, inviting, and more enclosed. This makes them ideal for expansive surfaces in overly large spaces but may be too constricting for small rooms. However, don't let this limit your choices. Keep in mind that the range of a single color offers multiple temperatures. For instance, if you like green, wheat grass is warm and elating while seafoam is tranquil and composed. Of course, the influence a specific color has on the feel of your room depends on the amount of the color you introduce. Using red to cover your walls or to simply detail a vase will influence your room's atmosphere in entirely different degrees.

PAGE 104
Lighting strongly influences this contemporary living room, which enlists muted tones and a wall of windows as the dramatic backdrop for its vibrant blue upholstery. At night, the room feels soulful and sultry, while during the day when the space fills with natural light, the mood becomes lively and animated.

OPPOSITE
Color is like a magnet that effortlessly draws the eye toward it. Set in a room of white, a bright orange wall frames a built-in cabinet making the colorful surface the room's dominant focal point.

USING COLOR TO ALTER SPACE

Color creates optical illusions that can change the look and feel of your living room. Determine your needs and let color do its work.

- If you want to delineate a zone like the sitting or dining area of your living space from the rest of the room, paint a single wall behind—or the ceiling above—the specific area with a contrasting color.

- If your living room is narrow, paint its longer side walls a lighter color than the end walls and the room will perceptually broaden.

- If your room suffers a low ceiling, paint the ceiling a light shade and it will recede skyward. Take this ceiling color and spread it just a little way down the walls, and the ceiling will seem larger while the room virtually expands as if you had moved the walls outward.

- If you want to automatically draw your eye through the room to give it depth, vividly color a wall at the end of the room or in a nook around the corner.

- If you want to incorporate colored pattern to affect the room's space, use vertical stripes to make a wall appear taller or horizontal stripes to make it appear wider. Running floorboards or a striped carpet across a narrow living space also broadens it. Square tiles placed diagonally across the floor stretch and expand the surface in every direction.

CHOOSING A COLOR

If you are planning to incorporate color into your living-room décor, here are a few tips to help you along the way.

- Every color has many looks, hinging on the texture of the surface, the room's lighting, and the amount of space the color covers. For this reason, analyze a color sample where you intend to use it.

- Apply a large enough sample—three- to four-feet square—to the intended surface in order to determine a color's look and feel. Remember that the larger the surface area, the more saturated or intense color appears.

- When testing a color, apply it to a white surface. Tinted surfaces can alter the way you perceive your test color.

- To properly test a color in different areas in the room and under different light, paint a sample on a movable piece of cardboard. Position it around the room and view it at different times throughout the day. Take it with you and use it as a guide when shopping for your living room's amenities.

- When deciding on the colors for your living space, consider the room's natural light. East- and north-facing rooms benefit from warmer tones of red, orange, and yellow because of the limited and cooler daylight they receive. West- and south- facing rooms, on the other hand, can accommodate cool tones of blue, green, and gray because their room's light warms the colors, making the room comfortable and inviting.

RIGHT
A bold chartreuse painting and a vivid red wall frame the opening to this great room's sitting area. Together, they constrict this walk-through region, making the white-walled living area into which they open appear more spacious and airy.

TEXTURE

Texture is a highly important detail to consider when designing your personalized living space. Sometimes overlooked and often taken for granted, texture is everywhere: in the sheen of a glass vase, in the nubby weave of a wool upholstered chair, in the sheer beauty of gauze draperies. Each material has textural qualities that enhance or detract from the feel of a space. The trick is recognizing the textural characteristic of an element and harnessing it to help shape the intended style of your living space.

When introducing textural depth to your room, enlist both the room's surfaces and its accessories. Overlook nothing. Creatively and ingeniously used, everyday objects and materials can become style-making additions to your room while influencing its spatial qualities as well. Heavily tactile objects make a space seem smaller—more comfortable and relaxing. Sculpted rugs, wooly throws, and rough organic accessories are naturally inviting and cozy. They entice one to experience the space, both visually and tactilely. Conversely, smooth stone, shimmering glass, and polished wood expand space while they create a restrained, more sophisticated setting. They are not as cozy but, for some, equally as alluring. Smooth or rough, hard or soft, glossy or distressed, texture brings a distinctive look to a room, personalizing it and making it more inviting.

Like color, texture touches everything, strongly influencing a room's ambience. Why not take advantage of its power to make the most of your living space? Texture flexes its muscle in many ways. In a living space used for everyday get-togethers and heavy entertaining, textured surfaces help to disguise spills and stains. Just like a patterned fabric, a highly textured surface camouflages a discoloration or blemish far better than a smooth surface. Because texture influences the way a color is perceived, it can bring spots of interest and life to even a monochromatic living space by creating multiple shades from a single color. Smooth, shiny textures intensify color, while rough, matte finishes subdue it. A lacquered black box appears darker and more powerful than a black chenille sofa. Both items feature the same color yet their textures create two different shades. Strong lighting intensifies this difference. This is important to remember when you choose matching and complementary furnishings, finishes, and fixtures.

PAGE 111
Texture can be used in place of pattern and multiple colors to bring character to a space. This sitting area uses a highly textured rock wall, a nubby woven throw, and grainy wood to enrich its muted color palette.

LEFT
Basketry, distressed wood, leather, and heavy woolens fill this casual space with a wealth of diverse textural interest.

OPPOSITE
In this mountain home, highly textured stone, wood, wool, iron, and reeds are played against the windows, a glass fire screen, and two oversized hurricane lamps. This room contrasts rough with smooth to dramatize texture.

The first step in introducing texture to your living space is determining the look and feel you want for the room. The next is selecting the materials to help you get there. Often texture implies a sense of temperature: grainy, nubby, and raised textures suggest warmth, while smooth and high-sheen textures feel cooler. For a high-impact look, use both.

Layer and contrast opposing textures: hard with soft, rough with smooth, shiny with dull. A silky satin looks luxurious when played against a coarse wool, while smooth glass sparkles against rough concrete and grainy wood. Play up the textural details of your living space, and you and your guests will naturally be drawn into it. A word of caution: be selective. Too many bold textural statements in a single space causes them to lose their impact.

OPPOSITE
Accessories provide an unlimited textural vocabulary for a room. Here, glowing candles and blown-glass vases contrast with the heavy weight and dark colors of metal stamping plates, iron sculptures, and a large metal brush. A whitewashed coffee table creates a neutral backdrop for the dynamic display.

UPPER RIGHT
Sleek, contemporary design calls for minimal textural statements. The waxed pine floors, a low-pile rug, a chrome-framed chair, and glossy white walls compose a low-tactile theme in this fashionable living space.

LOWER RIGHT
Nature provides inspiring examples of mixed textures. Here, raked plaster walls, a stone floor, a woven chair, and even a chip-carved table combine to shape the room's organic, relaxed ambience.

USING TEXTURE TO CREATE ATMOSPHERE

Introduce qualities of temperature by using texture. Create cool and calming ambience with smooth, shiny materials:

- Bamboo

- Chrome

- Ceramics

- Glass

- Glazed tile

- Glossy paint

- Marble

- Metal

- Mirrors

- Polished concrete

- Satin

- Sheer curtains

- Shiny granite

- Smooth silk

- Stainless steel

- Travertine

- Velvet

- Waxed woods

Create a warm and an inviting atmosphere with highly textured materials:

- Burlap
- Chenille
- Clay
- Brick
- Faux-fur
- Hammered nickel
- Knotty kilims
- Lamb's wool
- Limestone
- Linen
- Looped carpet
- Rough plaster
- Rusted iron
- Sisal
- Slate
- Suede
- Woven wicker
- Weathered wood

LEFT
A mixture of smooth materials—glazed ceramics, glass tabletop, and polished wood—help calm and refine the room's ambience that's animated by the highly textured flagstone flooring, chenille upholstery, and woven draperies.

Now that you have set the stage for your living room and determined a strategy for making the most of its space, it's time to furnish it with style, function, and a distinctive personality. This is where the room's "amenities" enter—the seating, tables, accessories, art. They make the room perform. They also influence its style.

To furnish the room so that it accommodates the way you live and reflects your own unique style, begin with the foundation pieces. Choose seating that anchors the room while providing comfort and character—maybe a sizable sofa or a circle of deep-seated armchairs. Place some benches or stools to provide extra seating and to perform as one-of-a-kind occasional tables. Augment them with strategically positioned end tables and perhaps a large cocktail table that amplify the room's style while creating a place for you to rest your drinks and place your cherished knickknacks and photos. Lastly, stage unique and colorful accessories, as well as art, to serve as the finishing touches that truly personalize the space.

As you furnish your living space, you will discover many choices that extend far beyond yesterday's traditional grouping of a sofa, two armchairs, and a pair of end tables topped with matching lamps. High-style living spaces now incorporate shapely chaises, boxy benches, oversized ottomans, and fabrics, finishes, and accessories that are purposefully mismatched to reflect individual and inspired design. Whatever combination of furnishings you select, it is important to keep their size proportionate to the room, and to position the pieces so the space feels balanced and so movement in the room flows smoothly. To fill the room with your signature style, incorporate prized collections, eye-catching accessories, and pieces of art that bring the room to life.

FURNITURE

Today's living space is the social hub of the home. It is where we congregate for relaxed family gatherings, get together to watch a movie or play games, settle in for intimate conversation, or simply curl up to enjoy a good read. A living space must be thoughtfully laid out and furnished to host all of these activities in comfort and style. Use seating and tables to create distinct conversation areas and special places that, for relaxation and leisure-time projects, help shape a room that addresses your needs and makes your time spent in the room a pleasure.

Like the living room, furniture has evolved to accommodate our desire to nest and spend more quality time at home. Where once a sofa, two chairs, and a suite of matching tables were the norm in the rarely used living space, we have now broken free from this restricted setup to choose pieces that specifically suit the way we live. If we prize lounging with the family in front of a large-screen TV, we often choose a large sectional centered around a similarly scaled cocktail table. If, on the other hand, we favor chatting with friends, we may be more likely to choose a couple of love seats or a circle of four chairs over the traditional sofa and matching armchairs. Today there are no rules. What's more, today's furnishings are selected to complement rather than duplicate each other in style, finish, and fabric. When an assortment of unique pieces is featured in the living room, a more personalized décor develops. Finally, we have begun to recognize the importance of flexible furnishings as they allow the multipurpose living room to adapt to our needs. Ottomans, benches, and stools serve as tables as well as footrests. Tables and chairs on casters allow us to move them around the room with ease, and modular-seating pieces can be repositioned to create varied arrangements as the need develops. Flexibility in furnishings and originality in furniture groupings can provide a fresh, fun look.

SEATING

Yesterday's unyielding, matching suite of sofas and chairs in no way serves the modern-day living room. Once staged for stiff, edge-of-your-seat entertaining or huddling around a monstrous TV console, upholstered furniture has outgrown these antiquated uses and settings. Now, multipurpose great rooms, family rooms, and entertainment areas are better served by upholstered furniture that accommodates the varied activities of the space. Consider how you use your space and let it influence the type of seating you incorporate into your living room. Customize seating to suit your room's layout, use, and character.

For everyday living, sofas continue to be a mainstay in most living rooms. They offer a lot of seating for one piece of furniture and also provide weight and mass that help balance a room's design. Before you decide on a specific sofa, consider its fit in the room and evaluate the many sizes and lengths available. If you are still uncertain, think beyond a sofa. Confined rooms benefit from one or two small love seats, while large great rooms often favor oversized sectionals. Their mass weights the space, and they are wonderful at defining the boundaries of a seating area. Often, sectionals are formed from modular units that can be arranged to custom fit your room in whatever size and shape you need.

The chaise lounge provides another alternative to the sofa. Styled something like a chair, but with a seat extended the length of a small sofa, the chaise's silhouette is less bulky than a sofa's and is therefore better suited in compact spaces. But remember, chaises are not fashioned to seat as many people as a sofa at one time (they are luxurious for one-person lounging), and because they often are directionally designed to be right- or left-facing, they are not as flexible for changing furniture arrangements.

Then, of course, there are chairs. Armchairs, wing chairs, club chairs, slipper chairs—the list goes on. While they have always served as the perfect sidekicks for a sofa, they can be grouped to go it alone, forming a circle of high-style seating that defines a conversation area. This works best with easy comfortable styles, as more regimented forms may make your living space look like a commercial lobby or waiting room.

PAGES 118–119
A pair of Old World globes and a contemporary vignette combining framed art, flowers, and a glass-cylindrical lamp adds unique charm to this otherwise sedate space.

PAGE 121
A modern chaise sits where a sofa may have been used in the past. This chaise and a pair of fashion-forward chairs are supplemented by two generously sized built-in benches to provide plentiful seating in this clean, contemporary space.

OPPOSITE
This large living area contains two separate seating areas, each anchored by different sofas and chairs. Two distinctively dissimilar coffee tables are used to further distinguish the two groupings.

ABOVE
Chair and a large ottoman provide this room with seating that is both stylish and flexible.

EVALUATING SEATING OPTIONS

When selecting an upholstered seating piece, there are a number of considerations. By evaluating different aspects of your sofa, chair, or chaise before making a purchase, you will be seated in bliss for many years down the road. Be certain furniture complements—not competes—with your décor.

COMFORT

Comfort is a primary consideration. After all, if a sofa or armchair isn't a pleasure to sit in, why have it in your home? First, think about how you like to sit in a sofa or chair. If you like to fall into the piece and sink into deep cushions, look for a generously padded, low-armed sofa with multiple pillows. If, on the other hand, you like to sit forward and prefer more support, then a firmer, higher seat is a better choice for you. Sit in each piece you are considering and evaluate its feel. Lean back and evaluate its relative fit to your body.

- Do you sit too low or far enough back?

The backs of your legs should be supported, so it is important that you sit far enough back in the chair or sofa. If your feet don't touch the floor when you are sitting back, the piece is too deep-seated.

• Is the arm height comfortable?

Think about how you will use the piece most often and where your arms are most at ease. For instance, if you plan to read while seated in the piece, your arms should be relaxed—not too high or low—while supporting a book.

• Are the cushions too soft or hard?

This is a personal choice; some people like the plush feel of down and feathers, while others prefer a firmer sit. Just as Goldilocks discovered through testing each bed, you have to experience cushions that are too soft or too hard in order to find the one that's just right.

ABOVE
Stylish stools and a lounge chair accompany a sofa and love seat to shape an intimate conversation area. Varied seating options provide an assortment of comfortable choices for guests and family members.

STYLE

Style relates to the silhouette and design of the upholstered piece. Every sofa, chair, and chaise has a unique frame and a personality that may or may not be appropriate for your living space. For this reason, it is very important that you define the style of your room before purchasing its furnishings. Let the style of your home, its architecture, and its setting help guide your decisions. A Victorian parlor calls for a different sofa than an Arts and Crafts bungalow. Purchasing a sofa or armchair is a long-term investment for many people, so fine quality and timeless design are important. When shopping, don't be tempted by trendy contours, exaggerated shapes, or sensationalized details like tufting, pillows, skirts, and trims.

With every piece, look beyond the fabric (which you are likely to change throughout the years) and simply observe the frame. Does it have staying power? Will it complement or compete with your décor?

Remember that while a highly stylized piece may be intriguing today, it may become irritating later on. Also keep in mind that the larger an upholstered piece is, the more its style will influence the character of your room. A trendy sofa is more likely to overwhelm your room than a similarly styled chair.

FABRIC

Fabric is important both in terms of appearance and durability. While it puts a face on furnishings with color, texture, and pattern, it also helps determine the wear-and-tear that the sofa or chair can endure. There is a general rule when you are making a long-term investment in an upholstered piece of furniture: the larger a piece of furniture is, the less aggressive its fabric should be. Bold colors and patterns that are endearing on pillows or stools can become overpowering on a sectional or twelve-foot sofa. They can consume a room. Of course, all rules have exceptions. If you have a highly unique décor that calls for a gussied-up frame, a sofa costumed in strong patterns, heavy trims, and elaborate tailoring may be just what you need.

Be practical when selecting fabric; consider the kind of use your upholstery will likely receive. If you are selecting an elegant piece that will get minimal use and exceptional care, a fine silk or linen may be perfect. For casual living, however, durability and easy care are important. Textured and patterned fabrics don't show wear, stains, or soiling as much as smooth plain materials. Nubby chenilles, textured tweeds, woven jacquards, and even leather present viable, long-wearing options.

SIZE

Appropriateness of size refers to more than being able to get your new upholstered furniture through the door into your living room. It relates to its scale and how proportionate it is to the rest of the room. Take stock of your room before shopping for a new sofa or chair, and go to the showrooms equipped with a tape measure and the dimensions of your living space. When determining the maximum length for a sofa or sectional, factor in the end tables that will sit at the end of the piece (normally thirty to thirty-six inches), as well as the amount of traffic space needed to move around it (at least thirty inches).

In small spaces, consider using a love seat rather than a sofa or selecting slipper chairs or pieces with open arms or legs. If placed in front of a window, the height of a seating piece should not interfere with the view. When a piece is positioned in the middle of the living space, its back should not excessively impede the view throughout the entire space.

OPPOSITE
A roll-arm, tufted-back sofa anchors this conversation area, while an antique armchair adds character without heft. The chair's open legs keep the room light and airy, relying on the bold art and shapely sofa to act as the main focal points in the room.

TABLES

Cocktail tables, sofa tables, and accent tables offer stylish support to an active living space. But selecting them can be challenging. After all, the demands on tables are many. To establish your needs and the tables most suitable for you, first consider the types of tables available and the functions they serve.

COCKTAIL TABLES

The cocktail table primarily serves as the hub of a seating area surrounded by sofas and chairs. Its size and height vary according to its setting, the seating pieces it serves, and the functions it performs. In large great rooms, the coffee table has grown to enormous proportions, keeping scale with the vast space and the massive sofas and sectionals that surround it. This table holds stacks of books, pots of plants, displays of accessories, and frequently the resting feet of the people sitting around it. Conversely, smaller living rooms often feature modest cocktail tables that may not be much larger than a serving tray. For the most part, they simply establish a nucleus for the sitting space and a convenient place to set a cup of tea or magazine. Whatever style or size you choose, make certain there is enough room to walk between the table and the seating pieces around it.

SOFA TABLES

A sofa table, as the name indicates, most often sits behind a sofa and is approximately the same height as the sofa's back. If you have a sofa, love seat, or sectional that floats in the room rather than resting against the wall, a sofa table can help break up the view of the sofa's plain back. A wonderful place to display accessories, the sofa table also presents a spot to set a lamp providing ambient and reading light for those seated on the sofa.

ACCENT TABLES

Occasional or accent tables are the most versatile, and often the most used, tables in the living room. No active living space should be without them. These are small tables that multitask as end tables, lamp tables, and card tables. They can even be grouped together to form cocktail tables—a workable alternative to placing an enormous door-sized table in the center of a room. Because of their modest size, occasional tables can be easily moved about. At one

moment an occasional table may be put near a chair for a guest to set her drink on, then later be moved next to the hearth to hold a stack of books.

While versatility is the occasional table's virtue, its beauty lies in its variety. These tables come in every material imaginable and in endless shapes and sizes. As their name points out, they are accents for the room. Use them to introduce surprising materials, silhouettes, and colors to your living space. Formal living rooms feature less variety in table finishes than do more casual spaces. Let the style of your living room be your guide as you mix and match materials and finishes in your personalized space.

OPPOSITE
A broad mixture of pieces, from pedestals to stools, serve as accent tables and extra seating for this lively room.

ABOVE
A shapely table may functionally serve a space and its design adds dramatically to the room's aesthetics.

OTTOMANS, BENCHES & STOOLS

Ottomans, benches, and stools provide comfort, charm, and dimension. As a group, they add extra dimension to the room's furnishing. They are neither tables nor seating pieces, but a combination of both. An ottoman, for example, acts as comfortable footrest, a spot to place a tray of refreshments, or as extra seating when needed. It also add immeasurable and mobile charm to the room. Ottomans are available in unlimited sizes and styles that fit almost any décor. For some, a square tufted-leather piece with exposed legs may be ideal, while for others a smaller, round, skirted ottoman with a plushy cushion would be a better fit. The possibilities are many.

Benches offer the same features and benefits as ottomans, just on a smaller scale. They can be tucked under a console or sofa table and pulled out as needed for extra seating. In small spaces, they can perform double duty as undersized cocktail tables and supplementary places to roost.

Stools also provide a place to perch. Because of their petite size, stools also often work overtime as unique accent tables.

Whichever of these pieces you incorporate into your living space, you will immediately add character and versatility to your furniture arrangements. While it is unlikely that you will move an armchair or sofa around the room to accommodate casual get-togethers, shuffling cushy benches, handsome ottomans, and simple stools into position is no big deal.

USING FUNCTIONAL FURNISHINGS

From solid tables to cushy ottomans, a living room benefits from pieces that deliver surface space and versatility to its décor. When incorporating these into your home, consider the following tips.

- Use tables to assure there is always a convenient place to set a drink while sitting anywhere in the room.

- Keep your tabletops uncluttered, making certain the surface is large enough to place a cup of coffee or cocktail among tabletop displays of collectibles, floral arrangements, books, and magazines.

- Use the seat height of your sofa to help guide the height of your coffee table. The table should be easy to reach and, if you allow, a comfortable height upon which to rest your tired feet while seated.

- When placing a coffee table on top of a beautiful area rug, consider using a table with a glass top so the rug's pattern and colors can be seen through the table. Be aware that glass tables are hazardous around active children and readily show smudges and dust.

- Choose stable benches, tables, and stools. Flimsy tables, particularly if they are small, can be easily knocked over by pets, children, or an accidental nudge.

- Use round or oval tables and stools in tight quarters. They are more versatile and perceptually consume less space.

- Incorporate glass-topped and leggy tables in small rooms; they allow light to flow through them and take up less space visually.

- Place large ottomans on casters, making it easier to move them around the room as necessary.

- Use slipcovers to give ottomans and benches a fresh look. Add contrasting piping, fringe, tassels, skirting, or another embellishments to create a one-of-a-kind look.

OPPOSITE
In this handsome room, a large ottoman is strategically positioned for fireside seating. Nearby, two custom cushions turn the raised hearth into a built-in bench.

ABOVE
A distinctive bench provides a perch in front of the fireplace and can be moved around the space when extra seating is necessary.

FURNITURE ARRANGEMENT

For many of us, arranging the furniture in a living room is like putting together a life-size jigsaw puzzle. There are so many pieces to work with and a confined space in which they all must fit. However, unlike a puzzle, there are no rights and wrongs and certainly more than one way to pull a room together. With a few tips and a clear idea of the way you plan to live in the room, you can take the guesswork out of arranging the furniture in your space.

TAKE STOCK

First examine your living area and the furnishings you have to work with. These are your tools. Then consider the overall purpose and personality of the room and how many people will use it. Will the room require wide-open spaces for large gatherings, small intimate spots for solitude, or cozy inviting pockets for you and your family? Does the space allow only a single conversation area or does it open itself to multiple furniture groupings? It's very important that the room not only looks great and is a pleasure to spend time in, but that it functions well and accommodates your lifestyle and activities.

CREATE A FOCAL POINT

The starting point for actually placing furniture is to determine the room's primary focal point. This is the feature that immediately draws your attention when you enter the space. In many living spaces it is a handsome fireplace or a picture window offering a breathtaking view. If you don't have a strong focal point, you can create one using art, a dynamic cabinet or media center, or other eye-catching design elements. Once you have zeroed in on the focal point, you can play up the asset and give your space structure by centering your main furniture grouping around it. In large great rooms, you may need to locate primary and secondary focal points, around which you will create multiple seating areas for the room.

ESTABLISH TRAFFIC PATTERNS

The next step is to establish the room's traffic patterns. By creating and keeping traffic patterns clear, the room will flow easily and feel more comfortable. The room's doorways determine its primary traffic pattern. Leaving unobstructed paths from one door to the others makes the room's layout feel friendly and at ease. This may include interior entries, adjoining hallways, stairways, and doors to the yard or patio. Beyond these main pathways, focus on keeping movement unrestricted by maintaining two to three feet open for any other paths that guide you through the room and its furniture groupings.

START BIG

When you place your furnishings, start with the large pieces like the sofa, armoire, coffee table, and entertainment center. This is important because there are fewer possible spots in your room that will actually accommodate these items. Once you have positioned these pieces, the smaller items should fill in easily. Don't turn your furnishings into wallflowers by lining them up around the room's perimeter. While some pieces like bookshelves, large cabinets, and entertainment centers naturally gravitate to walls because they are too bulky for the center of the room, other lower furnishings like sofas, chairs, and accent tables can be used to form islands of interest when they are positioned in the center of the room. This creates intimate "inner" rooms and, by pulling furniture away from the room's perimeter, gives you more arrangement options, since you won't have to work with the fixed walls to create your composition.

OPPOSITE

This large seating area centers on a stone-topped cocktail table with mobile stools stored underneath. The individual pieces are kept close to maintain unified intimate feel, permitting guests to enter and move around the area easily.

CONVERSATION AREAS

In today's homes, a welcoming area where we spend quiet moments alone with a book, enjoy one-on-one conversation with someone important to us, and entertain family and friends is at the heart of the living space. This central point of activity is most often oriented around the room's main focal point and looks as well as performs like a room within a room. Here, socializing directs the purpose of the space, but the furnishings define it.

When designing a conversation area, use furniture like a sofa, a pair of chairs, a large table, or a bench to outline the area and separate it from other parts of the room. Choose your main seating pieces and center them around a coffee table or large ottoman. Avoid limiting yourself to the traditional sofa and two chairs. Instead, a pair of love seats positioned across from each other, or perhaps four armchairs circled around a coffee table, may be the answer for you. Remember that normally only two people sit on a three-seat sofa at a time any way. The type and amount of seating should depend on your style preferences and the number of people you need to accommodate. Of course, benches, poufs, and stools can be used to supplement your main seating. Include tables that are in reach of all of your seating pieces, and always make space for a floor or table lamp in areas where you will be reading. The scale of a seating piece should match the tables that serve it.

Finally, keep all of the furnishings within eight to ten feet of each other to allow people to comfortably converse when they are seated in the space.

OPPOSITE
Anchored by the fireplace, this casual grouping of four armless chairs invites relaxed conversation and the enjoyment of views through broad floor-to-ceiling windows.

RIGHT
Two matching large-scale stone tables front this handsome room's elongated sofa. A small bench offers additional seating.

CREATING BALANCED FURNITURE ARRANGEMENTS

Thoughtful furniture placement makes the most of a room's area and provides balance to the space. Some tips for avoiding a muddled or lopsided living space include:

- Mix pieces of varying size, height, and weight. Avoid placing all of the large pieces at one end of the room and the smaller ones at the other.

- Use glass-topped tables and open-legged upholstered pieces to counterbalance the bulk of heavy chests, entertainment centers, and large fireplaces.

- Feature pieces of varying heights around the room so your eyes move up and down as they travel around the space. Create statements of height with tall cabinets, floor lamps, potted plants, bookshelves, and strategically placed wall art.

- Be mindful of scale. If a single table is too small to sit at the end of a large sofa, group a number of small tables to compensate for the sofa's mass.

- Avoid lining furniture along the wall, making the room look like an open dance floor. Even if a sofa can't sit in the center of the room, pull it away from the wall to give it breathing room. You may even want to place a narrow sofa table behind it.

- Look beyond the frames of your furnishings and be attentive to their patterns and colors. Balance these throughout the space as well.

- Use accessories to add bulk to furnishings. Books on tabletops, pillows on chairs, and collections in shelves add visual weight to meek furniture.

- Angle furnishings in the room. This adds another dimension to the space, making it more relaxed and less structured.

- Rather than adding furniture pieces to balance a space, try removing some. Cluttered and overfurnished spaces are overwhelming and uninviting.

RIGHT
A tall pedestal, large painted canvas, and tall table lamps offset the lower profiles of the room's chairs and tables. Together they add height and the weight to the room contributing dimension and balance.

ACCESSORIES

The stage of your living room is set: the architecture and surfaces are established, the space arranged, the furniture placed. Yet, while your room functions well and feels comfortable, there is still something missing. It's the accessories. Without them, the room is incomplete. Accessories are the special details that finish a room, filling it with your personal and distinct style. In a vital living space, accessories are everywhere: the lamps on the tables, the pillows on the sofa, the collectibles on the shelves, the framed photos on the mantel. While these take on endless forms, what they all have in common is the visual and tactile characteristics they give the space.

In general, there are two types of accessories. Firstly, there are those that are purely decorative, like a glass orb that sparkles on a tabletop or a figurine displayed on a mantel. Such pieces are eye-candy, and their sole purpose is to add character and beauty to the room. Secondly, items such as plush pillows or shapely lamps perform functional tasks; yet when chosen carefully, they can bring as much style to the space as they do practicality. Before you spend time searching for decorative pieces for your living space, take a discerning look at your room's working accessories.

Are your existing accessories adding or detracting from the room's ambience? Since working accessories are functional necessities and must be in the room anyway, why not make them perform double duty and contribute to its style as well? A discriminating eye will recognize the possibilities: a new shade or base for a lamp, a fresh cover on a pillow, a stylish doorstop, handsome fireplace tools. The list goes on. Once you have exploited the style potential for the room's must-haves, then turn your attention to the decorative accessories. Choose and display pieces that have meaning to you, pieces that make you smile. Whether you select items gathered during travels, treasures collected through time, or simply pieces that charm you, they should reflect your passions and interests to make a room that is uniquely yours.

Selecting accessories is only part of the task of finishing your living space. The other is positioning them in the room. Before attempting to place your treasured items, take a careful look around your room and you will find podiums for your accessories at every turn.

TABLES

Tables are generally the first spot that most people consider when placing accessories. Lamp tables, consoles, and cocktail tables create wonderful stages for accessories. Every table has its own character, providing a statement of scale, material, and style. These, in turn, influence what looks best on top of the piece.

The larger and more weighty a table, the larger its accessories should be. Dainty items are best left for curios or small-scaled surfaces. If a table features a patterned surface, such as a boldly mottled marble, dramatically grained wood, or a motif-rich painted top, don't use it to display patterned objects or a multitude of small items (unless you position them on a solid tray). They will simply cause visual confusion against the table's busy backdrop. Instead, choose solid-colored objects and pieces that raise your eye off the patterned surface—taller items with simple finishes like statuary, vases, candlesticks, and lamps.

If you have a distinctively styled table such as an ornate French console or dainty Oriental side table, you can either choose accessories of similar character for display or select dramatically different objects creating a bold contrast. A heavily grained Arts and Crafts-style oak table is a natural backdrop for a collection of simple Rookwood pottery from the same era. When juxtaposed with a group of simply formed, modern crystal vases, the display can be equally appealing.

MANTELS

In many living rooms, the fireplace performs as the strongest focal point and its mantel is one of the room's most important stages for treasured objects.

Whether your mantel is made of rugged timber, a granite slab, or sculpted metal, it invites a bold display as well as the fragile and expensive pieces best placed out of reach of rambunctious children and pets. Think beyond the conventional oil painting

centered between two candlesticks. Mirrors, vases, framed photography, and sculptures, all can contribute to a boldly accessorized mantel. If you display dissimilar objects, connect them with a unifying element: the same color, era, or material will help create harmony in the display. Also keep in mind that the larger and higher the mantel, the larger the items displayed on it should be. Small pieces will be hard to see and create visual clutter. Of course, a mantel can also serve as the ideal pedestal for a single item that is especially meaningful to you.

SHELVES

While the style and character of tables and mantels influence the items they are best paired with, shelves provide an almost blank canvas for display. The objects rather than the undistinguished shelves take center stage for your personalized exhibit. Niches and alcoves are similarly neutral places to position your cherished collectibles And, unlike tables, they provide more-sheltered spots to place fragile and valuable items. If you are starting from scratch and are designing shelves or niches in your living space, think about what items you will position there and have the openings custom-designed to fit the specific objects. Leave enough room so the objects can breathe, but not so much that they appear undersized in the cavities.

PAGE 139
While the solid cherrywood walls and symmetrically placed lamps suggest formality in this sitting area, casually stacked books and framed art haphazardly placed against a trunk table indicate a much more relaxed style.

OPPOSITE
This collector's library provides a multitude of surfaces for display. The tops and interior areas of built-in shelves, a broad mantel, and assorted tabletops house cherished pieces. Orderly choreography of the items helps keep the room from appearing cluttered or messy.

COLLECTIONS

Nothing reflects the interests and passions of homeowners more than the objects they collect. A collection of items tells a story about what is important to those who gather them. Furthermore, when displayed in an organized and appealing manner, collections act as eye-catching accessories, creating lively focal points that personalize a décor.

The challenge to integrating cherished objects into your living room's décor involves arranging the pieces into engaging displays. Collections should be grouped in clusters rather than scattered throughout the room. This creates impact. Otherwise, the objects may add clutter and chaos to the space.

The simplest display involves a collection of like items. If you prize seashells, for instance, display them together to create a coherent statement of your passion. The trick is to not overdo it. Make certain you edit your collection so that the pieces are not only attractive as a group but can also be admired individually. Allow the items to breathe. If they look crowded or "piled-up," remove some of the shells and rotate them into the grouping throughout time. Choose pieces carefully and let the largest or most eye-catching piece anchor the arrangement. Assemble the others around it. This will help balance your display of similar items. Foremost, select items that intrigue and inspire you. Collections and displays should reflect your interests and passions, not those of a designer or showroom.

GROUPINGS

Arranging unlike items can be a bit trickier. To make a grouping of unrelated items appear cohesive, choose a theme. Whether it is color, material, shape, origin, or style, a theme can unify the individual pieces into an eye-catching gathering. For instance, a monochromatic grouping of red objects—a ceramic lamp, crystal orbs, a lacquered wooden box, marble obelisk—creates a singular statement of style because of the shared color. The varied materials and disparate items make the display interesting.

Arranging a pleasing composition also involves the relationship between the items. Often the best compositions include something tall, something of medium height, and something short. The differently sized pieces create a landscape something like a mountain range, in which the eye continues to move up and down while traveling across the horizon. A well-composed grouping causes the eye to travel from one item to the next, never resting too long on any single piece.

Repetition can be useful when arranging items. Placing a number of identical items, same color, or matching shapes can add rhythm as well as drama to a display. They act like exclamation points that punctuate the arrangement at different spots.

While there are helpful guidelines in creating memorable groupings, the rule is to use your instincts, as well as trial and error, when choreographing a collection of items. In the end, you will have a pleasing arrangement that adds to your room's personalized décor.

ARRANGING COLLECTIONS

Whether it's a stack of tortoiseshell boxes resting on a table or a pile of vibrant pillows plumped on the sofa, an artistic arrangement of accessories draws you into a room for a closer inspection and an admiring gaze. In fact, it is often the composition of the items as much as the pieces themselves that creates the appeal.

- Leave breathing room between items. The blank spaces add to the rhythm of the arrangement and help direct the eye to individual pieces.

- Position small pieces together in a group to make a stronger impact with the pieces.

- Display pieces on top or in front of a mirrored surface to double their visual impact.

- Create interesting variety in height and depth by positioning displays on books and boxes.

- Exploit the color and transparency of glass items by positioning them in front of a window, below a light, or on top of a glass table.

- Use trays to unite and anchor groups of items. Trays are especially appealing when used as the foundation for multiple small objects, for pieces displayed on a patterned surface, or for collections placed on glass tables.

- Avoid rigid symmetry and organized rows for displays positioned in a relaxed décor.

- Incorporate architectural remnants and tarnished silver to give an arrangement instant heritage and aged beauty.

- Mix multiple textures in your composition to make it more interesting and strengthen its impact.

- Revisit your display occasionally to incorporate something new and rotate out old items.

- Soften the stiff look of symmetrical compositions by incorporating an asymmetrical grouping of smaller objects within the overall display.

PAGE 142
Antiquity and a monochromatic beige and taupe color story unite these pillows, urns, and statuary into a single well-conceived composition.

PAGE 143
This casually elegant room uses deep alcoves and a stone-topped table to house its displays. The accessories are limited and large in keeping with the scale and style of the room. Small pieces would look out of place in this voluminous space.

ABOVE
This light pine table is topped with a model ship and obelisk while the three balls provide sheen. To form the display's carefree, airy feel, the collection is loosely arranged and positioned in front of a mirror.

OPPOSITE
Books and boxes create miniature pedestals for tabletop display. To balance the large scale of a brass lamp, this draped table enlists polished wooden boxes and hardcover books to create assorted heights for the arrangement.

ART

A blank wall is to an inspired homeowner as an empty canvas is to a talented artist. It simply begs for a display of color, form, and character. While leaving some walls bare will help keep your living room open and airy, most benefit from some form of art. The dilemma to many is first deciding what to hang on the wall. What type of art should it be? Remember that wall art is not restricted to painted canvases or framed watercolors. It can also include everything from tapestries to quilts, architectural remnants to masks, and photographs to decorative mirrors. Let the style of your living room inspire and select those items that best complement the overall feel of the space. For example, a richly woven tapestry is more suitable than a series of Ansel Adams photographs for the walls of an Old World-style living room.

The next question involves the number of pieces you display. Do you want to make a dramatic statement with a single large item—a painted canvas, a Navajo rug, an antique door—or feature a grouping of smaller photographs, framed etchings, an hand-carved plaques? Whichever you choose, keep the look simple and uncluttered to get the most effect from the display. After all, art should present a desirable place for your eyes to rest, not a disorganized or messy sight that undermines the room's décor.

When you hang art, use the wall behind it to strengthen the impact. In most cases, art benefits from a certain amount of blank wall space around it. This allows the piece to breathe. With multiple items grouped together, the amount of space left between the pieces will affect not only the expanse of the display but also its visual strength. The more densely grouped the items are, the more power they have to draw the eye to them. Also keep in mind that art and the walls that support it create the backdrop for other elements in the room. Select pieces that enhance and support the other details you have chosen for the space.

ART PLACEMENT

For many people, one of the most challenging parts of incorporating art into their living space is positioning it on the walls. Is it too high or is it too low? Maybe it's just right.

While instinct can help guide you, you can also look to art galleries and museums for inspiration. Think about how they hang their art in relation to how you view it. If you are standing in the gallery looking at a beautiful canvas, the art is hung directly in front of you so you can inspect it without stooping over or straining your neck looking upward. Along the same line, if art is intended to be viewed by observers seated on a bench or stool, it is placed lower on the wall. These same placement techniques can be practiced at home. As a rule, you should hang all art at eye level. The pieces examined while walking by should be hung at standing height; those viewed while one is seated in a sofa or chair should be positioned at seating height.

The size and intricacy of the art can also influence its placement. Large canvases, rugs, architectural remnants, quilts, and other sizable items can be hung high on a wall where their visual strength isn't diluted by distance. Conversely, smaller and more intricate pieces should be hung at a level where they can be closely inspected and admired.

PAGE 146
This simple sculpture and copper bowl of moss join with dramatic art to form a powerful focal point creating a dramatic backdrop that unites other elements in the living room.

PAGE 147
Two canvases are positioned to frame a narrow window. Enough black wall surrounds the paintings so each is viewed individually as well as together with the window they encase.

OPPOSITE
A large framed photograph fills the wall behind the tufted chaise, making it visible from any spot in the room. A series of painted images over the chair are hung lower so they can be enjoyed while one is sitting in the chaise or when walking by the vignette.

ABOVE
Large canvases can create dynamic focal points out of expansive blank walls. Here, a bold piece of art and a stylishly accessorized console introduce the living room space. The art is hung at standing height to allow passersby to inspect it.

SIZE

On its own, a large canvas attracts the eye with its massive statement of color and character. Smaller images, on the other hand, need to be grouped to create the same kind of impact. As with accessories, small pieces of art scattered around a room create clutter; but as a group, they can be just as powerful and appealing as a single large piece.

To create a display of small art that is cohesive and harmonious, group images using a common denominator. You may want to use similar matting or related subject matter like botanical prints or colorful landscapes. Use matching or like frames or feature the same type of media, whether it be watercolor, etchings, or photography. By relating the pieces to each other with a common element, the collection as a whole becomes united.

ABOVE
This vibrant canvas is positioned at the end of a living room, drawing the eye through the entire space into this inviting sitting area. As a backdrop, the painting heightens the composition of furnishings placed before it and accentuates their textures and colors.

OPPOSITE
A series of photographs are positioned in a grid display to form a dynamic focal point. It features identical frames and matting that helps unify the collection as a whole.

ARRANGING GROUPS OF SMALL ARTWORK

Position groups of multiple images can be challenging. A few tips that can help you create a display that is picture-perfect include:

- Arrange your artwork on the floor before hanging it on the walls. This allows you to adjust the arrangement before making nail holes in the walls.

- Establish the perimeters of your arrangement with the corner pieces, then fill in the center space. To draw the eye into the groupings, create a focal point in the center area of the arrangement, using one large piece or a series of related pieces.

- Cut out full-size paper templates of each piece of art and tape them on the wall where you intend to hang the actual pieces. Reposition them until you are satisfied with the arrangement. Hammer nails or hooks using the wire or brackets on the back of the images or art as your guides. Tear the paper from the wall, leaving the nails or hooks in place, and hang each piece where its corresponding template had been positioned.

- Position the smaller or more intricate images in the grouping at a level where they can be inspected closely.

- Paint a panel of color on a wall and hang your artwork within its boundaries. The colored backdrop will help unify the collection, draw the eye, and strengthen the artwork's impact as a focal point.

- If you are hanging art on plaster walls, apply a piece of transparent tape to the wall before hammering in the nail. This will help keep the plaster from flaking or cracking.

- Look beyond your walls when displaying multiple pieces. You can hang them on the front edge of shelves or prop them on a mantel, console table, or even the floor. Layer them for a casual, spontaneous look that can be changed out at a whim.

A room that resonates character and personality—that should be the vision and inspiration when creating your own one-of-a-king living space. Look beyond yesterday's definition of this versatile space and make it one that not only accommodates the way you live but also makes you smile every time you enter. Whether you prefer a calm and serene setting that performs as a quiet getaway or desire a vibrant space that serves an active household, today's living space can and should indulge your individual needs. Think outside of the box when choosing the surface treatments, furnishings, and accents for the space and always keep in mind the purpose you have determined for the space. Do this, and you will enjoy a room that truly deserves its name, a living space that really lives.

ABOUT THE AUTHOR

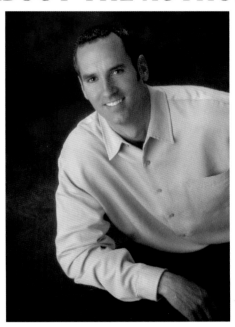

Brad Mee is a writer and author who specializes in home design. *Living Spaces: Design Is in the Details* is the sixth of a nationally renowned publication series he has created. It follows five other books that focus on interior and outdoor areas of the home. The series celebrates the power of detail in creating unique and beautifully personalized spaces. Brad is the editor of *Utah Style & Design Magazine* and divides his between his office in Salt Lake City, Utah and his home in Phoenix, Arizona.

I would like to thank all those who participated in making this book possible. Featured on every page is the work of extremely talented people. To the creative designers, architects, builders, and manufacturers whose talents are showcased throughout the book, thank you. Your work truly brings these living spaces to life. To the extraordinary photographers who captured the beauty of these rooms, I am indebted. My appreciation goes to the gracious homeowners who shared their living spaces and to my friends and colleagues at Chapelle, Ltd., for their continued support. Special thanks to my editors Karmen Quinney and Christine Allen-Yazzie. I am grateful to David Miller for sharing his dynamic work and to John and Margaret Mary Shuff for their encouragement. Finally, my sincerest thanks goes to photographers Dino Tonn and Scot Zimmerman for their friendships, their wonderful talents, and their contributions to this project.

ACKNOWLEDGMENTS

The author would like to thank the following for contributing photography to this book:

Dino Tonn Photography
5433 East Kathleen Road
Phoenix, Arizona 85254
(602) 765-0455

An attention to detail and true artistry in lighting have made Dino Tonn one of the leading architectural photographers in the Southwest. Specializing in award-winning architectural and golf-course photography, Tonn has been photographing much of the Southwest's finest architecture for the past fifteen years. He serves clients in the hospitality field as well as architects, interior designers, developers, and many other design-related businesses and publications. His work has been featured in regional and national publications. Tonn is a native of Arizona and resides in Scottsdale, Arizona, with his wife and two children.

Christiaan Blok–Photographer
(602) 667-5577
Phoenix, Arizona
www.cblok.com

A native of the Netherlands, Blok has pursued a career in architectural and interior photography. After graduating in 1990 form the Brooks Institute of Photography in Santa Barbara, California, he settled in Phoenix, Arizona, where he is currently based. He works worldwide for magazine and book projects and shoots on a regular basis for *Traditional Home, Southern Accents*, and *Phoenix Home & Garden*.

Lydia Cutter–Photographer
1029 North George Mason Drive
Arlington, Virginia 22205
(703) 741-0424

A specialist in interior photography, Lydia Cutter has been serving residential and commercial clients nationally for over twenty-three years. In addition to her photography, she also produces fine art that adorns beautiful homes and unique commercial buildings throughout the country. Her photographic work has been featured in national and regional publications. Cutter resides in Arlington, Virginia.

Bill Timmerman–Photographer
382 North 1st Avenue
Phoenix, Arizona 85003
(602) 420-9325

A professional photographer for twenty-seven years, Bill Timmerman's primary focus became architectural photography after his images of the Phoenix Central Library (architect Will Bruder) were published internationally. His ever-expanding clientele includes accomplished contemporary architects and interior designers. He has been a resident of Phoenix, Arizona, for eighteen years.

Scot Zimmerman–Photographer
P.O. Box 289
261 North 400 West
Heber City, Utah 84032-0289
(800) 279-2757/scotzman@sprynet.com
www.scotzimmermanphotography.com

Scot Zimmerman is an architectural photographer. During the last twenty-two years, his accomplishments include: photographing and producing seven books, having his photographs featured in over forty-eight books, regular contributions to national and regional architectural and home and garden publications, and ongoing assignments across the country. Six museums have exhibited his work.

David Michael Miller Associates
7034 East First Avenue
Scottsdale, Arizona 85251
(480) 425-7545
www.davidmichaelmiller.com

David Michael Miller Associates specializes in custom residential design and custom furniture design, from concept to completion. Miller, owner and principal, is committed to creating unique and beautiful environments for his clients. His sensitivity to organic materials, colors, and forms strongly influences his unique assemblage of art and objects. Miller's talent and projects have been recognized in interior design and home and garden magazines nationwide. His work has also been published in numerous interior design books.

Christopher K. Coffin Design
7500 E. McCormick Parkway Villa 4
Scottsdale, Arizona 85258
(480) 945-4080
cell: (480) 540-7724
fax: (480) 945-3311
www.christopher.coffin@att.net

Christopher K. Coffin Design focuses on high-end residential interior and exterior design with styles ranging from classic to contemporary styles that feature a mix of antiques with modern elements. Coffin's designs have been featured in nationally published magazines, along with local design-related television shows.

Kreiss Collection
1-800-kreiss-1
www.kreiss.com

The Kreiss Collection offers a singular blend of timeless inspiration and classic styling expressed in the finest materials, finishes, textures, fabrics and accessories. A Kreiss room mixes geographies and influences, with a style for every taste, every mood, every moment. Enjoy infinite possibilities for customizing your home beautifully—with Kreiss.

CREDITS

PHOTOGRAPHY

Christiaan Blok, Phoenix, AZ   54, 108–109, 128

Lydia Cutter, Arlington, VA   cover, 4–5, 7(r), 16–17, 22–23, 42–43, 45, 48, 56, 58–59, 60, 69, 77, 85, 96, 101, 116–117, 118–119, 127, 136–137, 148, 151

Bill Timmerman, Phoenix, AZ   1, 2, 3, 7(l), 8, 23 32, 33, 44, 49, 61, 68, 74, 84, 86-87, 91, 97, 112, 113, 130, 131, 149, 150, 155, 158, 160

Dino Tonn, Scottsdale, AZ   6(r), 21, 28–29, 34, 35, 36, 37, 38–39, 50–51, 53, 55, 62, 64, 66, 67, 70–71, 72–73, 89, 92–93, 99, 104–105, 121, 122, 124–125, 133

Scot Zimmerman, Heber City, UT   6(l), 12–13,14, 15, 18–19, 24–25, 26, 27, 30, 31, 38(ul), 41, 46, 65, 75, 76, 79, 81, 95, 100, 106, 111, 141, 145, 152–153

INTERIOR DESIGNERS

Anita Lang Mueller, Interior Motives, Fountain Hills, AZ   133

Billi Springer Interior Design, Scottsdale AZ   62

Christopher K. Coffin, Scottsdale, AZ   102–103

Cody Beal, Carlson Beal Interior Design, Salt Lake City and Park City, UT   95

David Michael Miller, David Michael Miller Associates, Scottsdale, AZ   1, 2, 3, 7(l), 8, 32, 33, 44, 49, 61, 68, 74, 84, 86-87, 91, 97, 99, 112, 113, 130, 131, 149, 150, 155, 158, 160

David Mitchell, David Mitchell and Associates Interior Design, Washington, DC   cover, 4–5, 7(r), 42–43, 45, 58-59, 101, 118–119, 127, 148, 151

Eric and Dorothy Bron, Bron Design Group Interiors, Phoenix, AZ   6(r), 50–51

Friedman & Shelds, Scottsdale, AZ   28–29, 64, 70–71

Jamie Herzlinger Interiors, Phoenix, AZ   121, 122

Jason Wilde, Harmon-Wilde Interior Design, Salt Lake City, UT,   14, 15, 145

Jill Jones, Split Rock Inc., St. George, UT   38(ul)

Jim Harris, J.W. Harris, Inc., Scottsdale, AZ   116–117

KEY
(l) = left
(r) = right
(u) = upper
(l) = lower

Jock Davis, Jock Davis Design Group, LLC, Alexandria, VA   60, 85

Justine Sancho Interior Design, Ltd., Bethesda, MD   16–17, 56, 96

Lamar Lizman and Liz Wixom, Lisman Richardson Interior Design, Salt Lake City, UT   18–19

Link Konizeski, deCondé's, and Lonnie Paulos, Salt Lake City, UT   75

Lisa Walker, Walker Design Group, Scottsdale, AZ   38–39

Liz Wixom and Tracee Goff, Lisman Richardson Interior Design, Salt Lake City, UT   24, 25

Magda Jakovcec, AIA , Jakovcev Architects, Salt Lake City, UT   81, 106

Melody Palmer, Quailwood Design, Bountiful, UT   65

Nancy Hepburn Interiors, Phoenix, AZ   53

Paula Berg and Amy Slaughter, Paula Berg Design Associates, Park City, UT and Scottsdale, AZ   111

Paula Berg, Paula Berg Design Associates, Park City, UT and Scottsdale, AZ   30–31

Peggy Fisher, Fisher Group, LLC, Annandale, VA   77

Peter Magee, Scottsdale, AZ   92–93

Rebecca Morse, Salt Lake City, UT   141

Robert Brain, Brainincorporated, and Patti Miller, Salt Lake City, UT   41

Robyn Shapiro, Robyn Shapiro Design, Chicago, IL   6(l), 12–13, 79, 152–153

Sharon Alber Fannin, Fannin Interiors Inc., 69, 136–137

Sherry Thompson, S Gallery, St. George, UT 38(ul)

Shirley Lyle Interiors, Purcellville, VA   22–23, 48

Teresa Kemp, Park City, UT   26, 27

Teri Mulmed, Do Daz, Inc. Design Firm, Scottsdale, AZ   34, 35, 36, 37

Vern Swaback, Studio V, Scottsdale, AZ   124–125

Vickee Byrum, Yellow Door Design, Austin, TX   100

ARCHITECTS

Abramson Teiger Architects, Culver City, CA
2, 3

Alan Tafoya AIA, Carefree, AZ   62

Bing Hu, H&S Enterprises, Scottsdale, AZ
98–99

Bob Bacon, RJ Bacon & Co., Phoenix, AZ
6(r), 50–51, 66

Charles Cunniffe, Charles Cunniffe Architects,
Aspen and Steamboat Springs, CO
30, 31, 111

Dave Richards, Salt Lake City, UT   26, 27

David Brems, Gillies Stransky Brems Smith,
Salt Lake City, UT   76

David Rohovit, The Rohovit Group,
Salt Lake City, UT,   18–19

DFD Cornoyer Hedrick, Phoenix, AZ   124–125

George Christensen, Brent Armstrong,
Vince Stroop, Scottsdale, AZ   8, 32, 33, 97,
149, 150, 158

H&S International, Scottsdale, AZ   104–105

Jack Plumb - Architectural Design,
Salt Lake City, UT   46

Kevin B. Howard Architects, Tucson, AZ   133

Magda Jakovcec, AIA, Jakovcev Architects,
Salt Lake City, UT   81, 106

Mark L. Neilson, Mesquite, NV,
ST. George, UT   38(ul)

Max Smith, MJSA Architects, Salt Lake City,
UT   41

Urban Design Associates, Scottsdale, AZ   53

BUILDERS

A.U. Construction (contractor), Salt Lake City,
UT   41

Al Coelho, Coelho Construction Company,
Park City, UT   111

Arnette-Romero Builders, Scottsdale, AZ   62

Ivory Homes, Salt Lake City, UT   24, 25

Juab Builders and Pelch & Richardson
(contractors), Salt Lake City, UT   75

Ken Keller, Keller Development,
Salt Lake City, UT   18–19

Kent Bylund, Split Rock Inc., St. George, UT
38(ul)

Legacy Homes, Scottsdale, AZ   8, 32, 33, 97,
149, 150, 158

Lowell Construction Company, SLC, UT
26, 27

Okland Construction, Salt Lake City, UT
81, 106

Phoenix Smith & Co. Inc., Scottsdale, AZ
28–29, 64, 71

Ren Boyce, Moenkopi Construction,
St. George, UT   38(ul)

Swaback Partners, Scottsdale, AZ   124–125

Todd Jensen and Brad Hayden, New Horizon
Homes, Salt Lake City, UT   46

Wall St. West Development, Scottsdale, AZ
104–105

CABINET DESIGN

European Design, Scottsdale, AZ   55, 72–73
124–125

MANUFACTURERS

Kreiss Collection, nationwide, 18(ul), 18(ll), 57,
82, 83, 103(lr), 110, 129, 134, 135, 138, 142,
143, 146, 147

PHOTODISKS

Corbis Corporation Images (© 2000) 114, 115(ur),
115(lr),

Photodics, Inc. Images (© 1999) 11, 20, 23(lr), 40,
47(ur), 52, 63, 78, 80, 88, 90, 98, 103(ur), 120,
139, 144

Every effort has been made to credit all contributors. We apologize in advance for any unintentional omission and would be pleased
to insert the appropriate acknowledgment in any subsequent edition.

Accent Tables 129

Access the Potential of Your
  Space 10

Accessories 78, 138–145

Amenities 118–151

Architectural Detail 62–65

Arranging Collections
  144

Arranging Groups of Small
  Artwork 150

Art 146–151

Art Placement 148–149

Assessment 10–11

Ceilings 60–67, 90

Choosing a Color 108

Cocktail Tables 16, 18, 92,
  94, 118, 120, 129

Collections 142–145

Color 71, 104–109

Comfort 124–125

Conversation Areas 135

Creating a Comfy and Casual
  Look 24

Creating a Detailed Ceiling
  67

Creating a Fresh Formal Look
  19

Create a Focal Point 132

Creating a Living-Room
  Retreat 49

Creating Balanced Furniture
  Arrangements 136

Decorating an Off-season
  Firebox 78

Defining Zones in a Great
  Room 32

Designing Shelves and Wall
  Niches 82

Entertainment Room
  . . . . 9, 34–39

Establish Traffic Patterns
  132

Evaluating Seating Options
  124

Fabric 126

Fireplaces 74–79

Floors 52–59

Formal Spaces 16–19

Furniture 1 20

Furniture Arrangement
  132–133

Great Room 9, 12,
  26–33, 56, 64, 67, 99, 108,
  123, 129,132

Hard Flooring 58

High Ceilings 90

Identify Problem
  Characteristics 10

Incorporating TVs into a Space
  39

Informal Spaces 20–25

Integration 71–73

Introduction 8–11

Large Spaces 92

Layering Light 99

Light 96–103

Living Room 14–25

Low Ceilings 90

Mantels 140

Material 71

Motif 71

Niches 68, 71, 73, 80,
  82–85, 99, 140

Ottomans, Benches & Stools
  130–131

Prioritize the Room's Pros &

Cons 10

Reflective Surfaces
  100–103

Rooms for Living 12–49

Scale 88–95

Seating 122–127

Shelves 80–85, 140

Size 126, 150–151

Small Spaces 94

Sofa Tables 129

Soft Flooring 59

Solitude 46–47

Space 86–117

Special Spaces 40–49

Surface Detail 67

Start Big 132

Style 126

Surfaces 50–85

Tables 128–129, 140

Take Stock 132

Texture 110–117

Using Color to Alter Space
  107

Using Functional Furnishings
  131

Using Rugs in the Living
  Room 56

Using Scale to Upsize a Small
  Room 94

Using Texture to Create
  Atmosphere 116–117

Walls 68

Workspace 42–43

INDEX